SpringerBriefs in Public Health

SpringerBriefs in Child Health

Series Editor
Angelo P. Giardino, Department of Pediatrics, 2S010
University of Utah
Salt Lake City, UT, USA

SpringerBriefs in Child Health present concise summaries of cutting-edge research and practical applications from the fields of child and adolescent health. This book series is designed to target children's health issues from birth through adolescence, from both a policy and practice perspective. Each subject in the series will be written by a specialist in that area. Their expertise will offer evaluation of the special health issues that would be of value to any health care provider. The authors all practice at nationally recognized children's hospitals and have done extensive research in their respective areas. The "template" for the series will be in three sections:

- "Snapshot from the Field" will address current practice and policy
- "Implications for Policy and Practice" will deal with the emerging science and best practices related to cutting edge work going on in the field
- "Looking Ahead" will look forward towards anticipated changes, recommendations and strategies to achieve the best for children and families.

Featuring compact volumes of 55 to 125 pages, the series covers a range of content from professional to academic. Possible volumes in the series may consist of timely reports of state-of-the art analytical techniques, reports from the field, snapshots of hot and/or emerging topics, elaborated theses, literature reviews, and in-depth case studies. Both solicited and unsolicited manuscripts are considered for publication in this series. Briefs are published as part of Springer's eBook collection, with millions of users worldwide. In addition, Briefs are available for individual print and electronic purchase. Briefs are characterized by fast, global electronic dissemination, standard publishing contracts, easy-to-use manuscript preparation and formatting guidelines, and expedited production schedules. We aim for publication 8-12 weeks after acceptance.

Kaitlyn Sacotte • Brandon Tomlin
Allison Judkins • Luca Brunelli

The Evolution of Global Child Rights

Protecting the Vulnerable

With Contributions by Stephanie Persson and
Meredith Giovanelli

Springer

Kaitlyn Sacotte
Division of Neonatology
Department of Pediatrics
Spencer Fox Eccles School of Medicine
University of Utah Health
Salt Lake City, UT, USA

Brandon Tomlin
Division of Neonatology
Department of Pediatrics
Spencer Fox Eccles School of Medicine
University of Utah Health
Salt Lake City, UT, USA

Allison Judkins
Division of Neonatology
Department of Pediatrics
Spencer Fox Eccles School of Medicine
University of Utah Health
Salt Lake City, UT, USA

Luca Brunelli
Division of Neonatology
Department of Pediatrics
Spencer Fox Eccles School of Medicine
University of Utah Health
Salt Lake City, UT, USA

ISSN 2192-3698 ISSN 2192-3701 (electronic)
SpringerBriefs in Public Health
ISSN 2625-2872 ISSN 2625-2880 (electronic)
SpringerBriefs in Child Health
ISBN 978-3-031-45519-3 ISBN 978-3-031-45520-9 (eBook)
https://doi.org/10.1007/978-3-031-45520-9

This Springer imprint is published by the registered company Springer Nature Switzerland AG
The registered company address is: Gewerbestrasse 11, 6330 Cham, Switzerland

Paper in this product is recyclable.

This book is dedicated to all those who, by respecting the rule of law, pursuing social justice and peace, and seeking the truth for the common good, serve as role models on how to protect children's dignity and advance their rights.

Foreword

As we celebrate the 100th anniversary of the adoption of the Declaration of the Rights of the Child [1], it is fitting that we both reflect on the principles that underlie this groundbreaking statement as well as consider what we can do now, 100 years later, to more fully realize the aspirations so nobly stated in 1924 [1]. The child health advocates who authored this monograph provide us with a solid foundation in Chap. 1 upon which to base this reflection anchored in philosophy, history, and policy analysis. Professionals and members of the general public who are interested in optimizing the health and well-being of children in our society are ideally situated to serve both individually and collectively as stewards of the childhoods for all the children and adolescents in our neighborhoods, broader communities, and within and across nations across the globe. This stewardship obligation is reflected in the comments of prominent child advocates such as Dr. Melissa Merrick, CEO for Prevent Child Abuse America, who frequently reminds us in her public addresses that "childhood lasts a lifetime" [2]. This simple statement encapsulates the life-course perspective so important to our understanding about the centrality of the early years of a person's life, i.e., one's childhood, in promoting optimal development and well-being as a child as well as long afterward in one's adulthood.

As we learn more about child development and what factors promote safe, stable nurturing environments, we can improve our policies and practices such that all children have the opportunity to develop their full potential in an environment that supports and encourages them. The notion of ongoing improvement based on an ever more refined understanding of what entails a growth-promoting environment for children and adolescents is woven into the DNA of this monograph and immediately reminds us of the call to action from poet-laureate Maya Angelou about being committed to always improving as we learn more: "Do the best you can until you know better. Then when you know better, do better" [3]. The more we recognize what helps children develop their full potential, it seems fitting that professionals and the general public should commit themselves to do better!

Among the many key takeaways from this monograph is the detailed discussion in Chap. 2 about a human dignity framework which revolves around a community's respect for the inherent value of each of its members. This discussion and its connection to a child's human rights and our evolving understanding of a child's health provides a firm foundation upon which one can move forward toward policies and actions aimed at the creation and maintenance of safe, stable, nurturing environments so essential to the optimal development of children as they move through their childhoods. Then, in Chaps. 3 and 4, the authors lead us as readers through a deep dive into the factors that underlie human dignity related to US health, health care, and child welfare systems. Chapter 5 provides us with a global perspective on child health, child rights, and human dignity and gives the reader a deeper understanding of the United Nation's Convention on the Rights of the Child. The concluding Chap. 6 challenges child advocates in general, and pediatric professionals specifically, to step-up and take on the stewardship, in Angelou's words, to "do better" now that we "know better" [3].

Looking back to 1924, much work was set before the child advocates of the time, and now, 100 years later, despite a lot of effort and many improvements with regard to children and their rights, much work remains to be done. This monograph provides the fuel to ignite our action to set about doing this work. The human dignity framework provides the contours that can shape our imagination about what could, and should, be possible to safeguard children and their childhoods within our communities throughout the globe. Let's hope we don't need another 100 years to make the gains we need to ensure that all children are valued as members of our society and provided with the supports and encouragements necessary and sufficient to ensure a safe, stable, nurturing environment from which they can emerge and realize their full potential.

Angelo P. Giardino, MD, PhD

Wilma T. Gibson Presidential Professor
Chair, Department of Pediatrics
University of Utah School of Medicine
Salt Lake City, UT, USA

Chief Medical Officer
Intermountain Primary Children's Hospital
Salt Lake City, UT, USA
August 28, 2023

References

1. Geneva Declaration of the Rights of the Child. In: UN documents: gathering a body of global agreements. n.d. http://www.un-documents.net/gdrc1924.htm. Accessed 25 Aug 2023.
2. Merrick M. A message from Dr. Merrick on shifting the narrative to child and family well-being. In: Prevent child abuse. 2021. https://preventchildabuse.org/latest-activity/shifting-the-narrative-to-child-family-well-being/. Accessed 25 Aug 2023.
3. Angelou M. [@DrMayaAngelou]. Do the best you can until you know better [Tweet]. Twitter. 2018, August 12. https://twitter.com/DrMayaAngelou/status/1028663286512930817?lang=en

Contents

About the Authors

Kaitlyn Sacotte, MD, is a Neonatal-Perinatal Medicine fellow at the University of Utah. She attended Northwestern Feinberg School of Medicine for medical school and completed her pediatrics residency at Oregon Health and Science University before moving to Utah. Her research interests have centered around adverse childhood experiences and social determinants of health and their effects on health. Dr. Sacotte's work has been published in journals such as *JAMA Network Open* and *Journal of Adolescent Health.*

Brandon Tomlin, MD, obtained his bachelor's in biomedical engineering at the Milwaukee School of Engineering and then attended medical school at the Medical College of Wisconsin. He completed his residency in pediatrics at the University of Wisconsin Madison and stayed an additional year to serve as Global Health Chief Resident. He is currently in his third year of his perinatal-neonatal medicine fellowship at the University of Utah. His research interests are in medical device development, specifically for global health applications.

Allison Judkins, MD, is passionate about improving the care of our most vulnerable populations, both in the United States and abroad, and sharing that passion with others through medical education. She has the privilege of doing just that in her clinical career as an academic neonatologist at the University of Utah, caring for our most fragile babies, and training the next generation of physicians to do the same. She has been the site lead in both India and Nepal for the last 5 years for ongoing health-care improvement projects, including Helping Babies Breathe (HBB) initiatives as well as successful community-based educational initiatives in caring for high mortality populations, including low birthweight infants. Currently, she is working with academic partners in Nepal developing a sustainable HBB/Helping Mothers Survive (HMS) dissemination in Nepal's most remote settings, as well as a quality improvement project assessing neonatal hypothermia and thermal care practices in the same regions. She has had the privilege to lead teams of students in multiple quality improvement and educational projects in collaboration with the governments and experts in Nepal and India, and mentor them through the delicate process of conducting sound, sustainable, collaborative projects with local partners. Through this work, she has been able to collaborate with the AAP in global educational and QI efforts, including the implementation of Essential Newborn Care (ENC) Now in Bangladesh and Nigeria, and Project ECHO in Ethiopia. In her free time, she enjoys spending time outdoors in beautiful Utah with her husband and children.

Luca Brunelli, MD, PhD, is Professor of Pediatrics in the Division of Neonatology at the University of Utah. After completing pediatric and anesthesia residencies, he worked as a pediatric anesthesiologist at Gaslini Children's Hospital in Italy and led a medical mission to the Philippines. After moving to the United States, he completed a pediatric residency at the University of Rochester, and a neonatology fellowship at Duke University and Thomas Jefferson University. Dr. Brunelli's research interests have spanned from mouse and human genetics to genetic engineering and children's rights to health and wellbeing, publishing in journals such as *Circulation Research*, *Molecular and Cellular Biology*, *JAMA Pediatrics*, and *Nature Methods*. His research has been funded by the American Heart Association, the National Science Foundation, and the National Institutes of Health. He has co-chaired the Genomics Focus Group at the Children's Hospital Neonatal Consortium as well as the Bioethics and Legal Workgroup at the Newborn Screening Translation Research Network of the American College of Medical Genetics and Genomics. He is currently pursuing a master's in philosophy (ethics).

Contributors

Meredith Giovanelli, MPH Children's Rights, New York, NY, USA

Stephanie Persson, JD Children's Rights, New York, NY, USA

Chapter 1
A Brief History of Children's Rights

As with any venture in public health, to make any advancements as a society is to examine and learn from the past. In the case of progressing children's rights, there is a long and storied history to the subject. However, it is not quite as long as one might expect. While children have been around for the entirety of humanity, they have not always been viewed in the same way they are today. The viewpoint that children are a population that should be protected and held to a separate set of standards than adults is a relatively new concept. In fact, the first federal government action protecting children from exploitative labor in the United States did not take place until the twentieth century. Fortunately, many countries around the world have come to recognize the vulnerability of children and the need for their protection, demonstrating an evolution of priorities and values. The laws and declarations described in this chapter are proof to that effect. However, the United States has fallen behind in key areas and in some respects is taking steps backward compared to the rest of the world. This is why looking critically at our past is more important now than ever if we wish to continue advocating and advancing the rights of children.

History of Childhood

Before diving into the history of children's rights, it is necessary to look at the history of children themselves, not as an age group but rather as a concept. Most civilizations have had some transition point between infancy and adulthood. Looking simply at the ubiquity of coming-of-age ceremonies throughout the world, it can be deduced that most civilizations had an idea of "adulthood." Early Western definitions of childhood were proposed by Aristotle who saw the concept of the child as a being who is important for their potential, not for themselves. Dante defined childhood a bit more concretely with the division of a man's life into three periods: *adolescenzia* or adolescence (up to age 25), *gioventute* or youth (25–45), and *senettute*

K. Sacotte et al., *The Evolution of Global Child Rights*, SpringerBriefs in Public Health, https://doi.org/10.1007/978-3-031-45520-9_1

or old age (45 to about 70) [1]. One of the first historians to study this concept was Philippe Ariès, a French historian who wrote *Centuries of Childhood.* He came to the conclusion that the idea of childhood is a relatively modern idea that came into emergence after medieval times. Using medieval artwork as a major source of his assertations, he argued that in those times, children were treated like small adults and detached from the family [2]. While his methods have been criticized and conclusions disputed, what can be certain is that the *experience* of childhood varied widely by region and class level of the parents.

There are varying theories about when the concept of childhood was conceived. While some postulate that the Puritans in England were the first to believe children were more than just "filthy bundles of original sin," [3] others claim it was first recognized in the late seventeenth century in Russia where educational primers on grammar and religion appear targeted toward youth [1]. John Locke himself alluded to the conception of childhood in his 1693 work *Some Thoughts Concerning Education* where he compares the son of the gentleman for whom it was written "only as white as Paper, or Wax, to be moulded and fashioned as one pleases" [4]. Regardless of when it was first defined, a group of Enlightenment thinkers in the eighteenth century challenged the idea of original sin in children and rather posited that childhood is a time of innocence. Later, Romantic thinkers fought for childhood to be a time for positive education in the creation of the adult self [1]. Childhood became better defined throughout the nineteenth century. The two-volume work called *Adolescence* by the psychologist G. Stanley Hall brought much needed clarity to the concept as well as extended this life stage up to 24 years [5]. He defined adolescence itself as a time of "storm and stress" during which the adult mind was still developing.

Child Labor

Along with the concept of childhood, laws surrounding child labor followed, albeit with some delay. Children have been part of the workforce for as long as humans have formed communities. The work generally involved age-appropriate tasks that helped promote the survival of the group. This was especially important given the high mortality rate of children in the preindustrial era, as those who helped the tribe survive were more likely to survive themselves. Recently discovered skeletal remains hint that some children as young as eight may have worked laborious jobs such as mining or brickmaking [6]. In the medieval era, when literacy was a skill needed by relatively few, the act of working or apprenticeship was a more meaningful form of education that would provide the skills necessary for survival as the child moved into adulthood. This system worked well for the time, but as the world moved into the industrial revolution, two key forces played fundamental roles to drive change. First, the improvement in income, manufacturing, and medical practices in the cities led to a dramatic decrease in childhood mortality [7]. Second, capitalistic pressures demanded upscaling manufacturing, which increased the need for large amounts of cheap labor. The combination of these two forces led, in a predictable way, to the employment of children, not to learn a meaningful trade but to cut manufacturing costs. Author Upton Sinclair summarized this point in his novel *The Jungle*:

> *Very often a man could get no work in Packingtown for months, while a child could go and get a place easily; there was always some new machine, by which the packers could get as much work out of a child as they had been able to get out of a man, and for a third of the pay* [8].

Along with the increase in labor during the Industrial Revolution, there began a shift in thinking around child labor from being a source of education and preparation for adulthood to being a form of exploitation. The first laws in the United States around child labor were at the state level and remained modest but were small steps toward larger reform. In 1813, Connecticut passed a law that required children who worked in factories to be educated in mathematics, reading, and writing. In 1842, Massachusetts imposed a workday limit for children under 12, stating they could not work longer than 10 h a day in factories [9]. Similar state legislation throughout New England was scattered through the nineteenth century, but the move for larger reform came with the rise of the Prohibition Party in 1872, which included condemning child labor as part of their platform [10]. Laws continued to curtail child labor in the northern states through the end of the nineteenth century, and laws requiring education for children were beginning to be enacted in the South during post–Civil War reconstruction [11].

Reforms truly became mainstream in the early twentieth century as a growing body became interested in pushing legislation at a federal level, and, with the foundation of the National Child Labor Committee (NCLC) in 1904, there was finally an organized advocacy group for child laborers [10]. Manufacturers began to shift from viewing children as assets, too, noting that while adults require higher wages, productivity increases, and rates of accidents decrease enough to make up for it. By 1906, a majority of manufacturers did not think child labor added value to their buisness [12]. The NCLC believed that the most judicious path forward was to push legislation at the federal level; through their efforts, the first major federal labor bill was introduced to Congress in 1906, which would prohibit the interstate transport of goods mined or manufactured by those under the age of 14. This bill unfortunately failed, but progress continued at a state level with more laws establishing minimum working ages, though the enforcement was lax [13]. The first major federal legislation to pass was the Keating-Owen Child Labor Act of 1916. This bill was drafted with the assistance of the NCLC and proposed that the minimum age of factory and workshop workers be 14 and mine and quarry workers be 16. It also prohibited night-time work and established an 8-h-a-day workday limit on workers under 16 [14]. While this was a major accomplishment, its effects were short-lived. The Keating-Owen Child Labor Act was deemed unconstitutional by the Supreme Court in 1918 as they viewed the Act as the federal government overstepping its powers to regulate interstate commerce [14].

Little progress was made in the subsequent years, and child labor continued to be widespread. There was an attempt at a constitutional amendment to outlaw child labor which failed, and President Franklin D. Roosevelt endeavored to eliminate child labor using executive action, but this also failed. It wasn't until the Fair Labor Standards Act (FLSA) of 1938, a bill modeled after the Keating-Owen Act, that federal legislation was upheld by the Supreme Court. Similar to the Keating-Owen Act, the FLSA prohibited interstate commerce of goods that used child labor in their production and increased the minimum age of child workers to 16 in nonhazardous environments and to 18 in hazardous environments. Among the provisions of this Act were the first minimum wage of $0.25 per hour, overtime pay if working over 40 h per week, and the creation of the Department of Labor's Wage and Hour Division as an enforcement branch [15]. With the passage and upholding of the FLSA, the United States made a clear statement on its priorities around child labor. Fortunately, the FLSA has stood the test of time, with it still being in effect today.

Of course, alongside all of this progress, childhood labor among slaves in the United States was routine and expected. This underwent little scrutiny until after the Civil War during Reconstruction. Additionally, the reforms mentioned focus on the laws enacted in the United States, while child labor was and continues to be a major issue in other countries around the world. While it is imperative to work toward the fair and humane treatment of children, it is important to understand the limitations of a country's ability to impose its values on another country.

International Law

The principal way that multiple countries agree on a set of laws or practices is through international law. At a basic level, international law takes two major forms: international treaties and customary international law. Comprehension of the basics of these legal principles is important in order to grasp the landscape of international child rights treaties and what enforcement is available for any apparent violations.

Modern treaties were defined at the Vienna Convention on the Law of Treaties, which was drafted by the International Law Commission of the United Nations (UN). Work on this convention began in 1949, but it wasn't officially adopted until 1969. It specifies that a treaty is "an international agreement concluded between States in written form and governed by international law, whether embodied in a single instrument or in two or more related instruments and whatever its particular designation," where instruments are the relevant international conventions or resolutions [16]. When a treaty is drafted, it must pass two steps before it can become enforceable. The first step is signing on to the treaty, where all countries who are creating the treaty sign as an approval of the language of the document. This, however, does not mean that the countries agree to the terms of the treaty, but rather that they agree with the sentiment or principles written within. To legally agree to the terms of a treaty, it must be ratified by their government. In the United States, this is done by the Senate where two thirds of the body must vote in favor of the treaty.

Enforcement of international treaties is up to each country on its own and is categorized according to two principles. The first principle is monism, where a country declares that international and national law are a part of the same legal system, and therefore hold the same weight in the court of law. The second principle is dualism, where international law must first be converted into a national law before it can be enforced. The United States is a complicated mix of both principles, where Article VI of the constitution states that treaties are part of the "Supreme Law of the Land," but the Supreme Court has ruled that treaties that do not contain a "self-executing" clause must be first implemented by a governing body after ratification [17].

Customary international law is a little different and much less rigid, in that it is defined by general practices accepted as laws. A customary practice requires two elements to be considered international law: sufficiently general state practice and *opinio juris.* Sufficient state practice means that a majority of countries and great powers follow a practice out of legal obligation [18]. *Opinio juris,* which is a Latin phrase that translates to "an opinion of law," in practice means that the country in question feels a subjective obligation to follow a particular law [19]. While some of these customs have been codified into international law through treaties, most of these customs are considered so widespread that if a country has not officially objected to the law, they can be considered bound by it. One can imagine that this type of law is difficult to identify and enforce, but it does play an important role when a country interacts or confronts a non-state actor. For example, in the case *Prosecutor v. Kayishema and Ruzindana,* the international court found the two defendants guilty of genocide during the Rwandan Civil War, the practice of which had been decried as a violation of both customary law and the Convention on the Prevention and Punishment of the Crime of Genocide.

Establishing Rights for Children

So, what has been done by the international community to protect the rights of children in the past 100 years? A few key documents emerged that were integral to child protection efforts. The first of these documents was the Declaration of the Rights of the Child, adopted by the League of Nations nearly 100 years ago. The push for this declaration was spearheaded by *L'Union Internationale de Secours aux Enfants*, or the International Save the Children Union, which was founded in Geneva in 1919. The Union's goal was to end child suffering in Europe after World War I, part of which included drafting the Declaration of the Rights of the Child in 1923 and quickly lobbying for its adoption by the League of Nations in 1924 [20]. The text of the Declaration is simple and is as follows:

> *By the present Declaration of the Rights of the Child, commonly known as "Declaration of Geneva," men and women of all nations, recognizing that mankind owes to the Child the best that it has to give, declare and accept it as their duty that, beyond and above all considerations of race, nationality or creed:*

1. *The child must be given the means requisite for its normal development, both materially and spiritually.*
2. *The child that is hungry must be fed, the child that is sick must be nursed, the child that is backward must be helped, the delinquent child must be reclaimed, and the orphan and the waif must be sheltered and succoured.*
3. *The child must be the first to receive relief in times of distress.*
4. *The child must be put in a position to earn a livelihood, and must be protected against every form of exploitation.*
5. *The child must be brought up in the consciousness that its talents must be devoted to the service of its fellow men* [21].

This was a major step forward for the international community in the acknowledgment that children need to be cared for and protected. However, the word "right" is not mentioned anywhere in the text of the declaration. This was addressed after World War II and the formation of the United Nations. They saw the need to update and adopt an official UN Declaration to address childhood rights. Based on the original declaration of 1924, the United Nations passed the revised Declaration of the Rights of the Child in 1959. This document kept the underlying spirit of the 1924 declaration that the world owes children the best mankind has to give but expanded to 10 principles and describes them as "rights" rather than acts that mankind must do to protect children. These principles are summarized here:

1. All children without any exception shall be entitled to the rights in this declaration.
2. The child shall have special protection and opportunities to develop in a healthy and normal manner.
3. The child shall be entitled from his birth to a name and nationality.
4. The child and his mother shall have the benefits of social security including pre- and postnatal care, nutrition, housing, recreation, and medical services.
5. The child who is handicapped shall be given the care required by their condition.
6. The child shall not be separated from their mother except for extraordinary circumstances, in which public authorities will care for the child.
7. The child is entitled to a free education, which includes opportunity for play and recreation.
8. The child shall in all circumstances be among the first to receive protection and relief.
9. The child shall be protected from neglect, cruelty, and exploitation. They cannot be employed before an appropriate minimum age and cannot engage in work that interferes with their development.
10. The child shall be protected from any form of discrimination [22].

While this document had much stronger language than the 1924 declaration, its main shortcoming was that it was not a legally binding resolution, but rather a list of rights countries should strive for. The first legally binding set of rights that included children was the International Covenant on Civil and Political Rights (ICCPR) and the International Covenant on Economic, Social, and Cultural Rights (ICESCR). These two resolutions were human, not child, rights that protect against slavery, forced servitude, torture, and inhumane punishment [23]. However, Article

24 of the ICCPR does specifically provide that all children have the right to protection as a minor, and also shall have a name and nationality [24]. The ICESCR protects the child through protection of the rights of the family [23]. While neither of these documents were specifically written for the rights of children, they did have broad appeal, with 130 nations signing on, and these documents have been used in cases protecting the rights of juveniles [23].

As part of a celebration of the 20th anniversary of the 1959 declaration on the rights of the child, the United Nations determined in 1979 that an updated declaration should be drafted, one that not only includes special rights for the child but would also be legally binding. A working group was formed in 1979 to write the Convention on the Rights of the Child (CRC). Work on this document would take place over the next 10 years until it was presented to the United Nations General Assembly in 1989. The text of the document includes 54 separate articles and two optional protocols. A list of the articles is as follows:

1. Definition of the child
2. Nondiscrimination
3. Best interests of the child
4. Protection of rights
5. Parental guidance
6. Survival and development
7. Registration, name, nationality, and care
8. Preservation of identity
9. Separation from parents
10. Family reunification
11. Kidnapping
12. Respect for the views of the child
13. Freedom of expression
14. Freedom of thought, conscience, and religion
15. Freedom of association
16. Right to privacy
17. Access to information; mass media
18. Parental responsibilities; state assistance
19. Protection from all forms of violence
20. Children deprived of family environment
21. Adoption
22. Refugee children
23. Children with disabilities
24. Health and health services
25. Review of treatment in care
26. Social security
27. Adequate standard of living
28. Right to education
29. Goals of education
30. Children of minorities/indigenous groups

31. Leisure, play, and culture
32. Child labor
33. Drug abuse
34. Sexual exploitation
35. Abduction, sale, and trafficking
36. Other forms of exploitation
37. Detention and punishment
38. War and armed conflicts
39. Rehabilitation of child victims
40. Juvenile justice
41. Respect for superior national standards
42. Knowledge of rights
43–54. Implementation measures [25]

The United States played a major role in the drafting of the convention under both the Reagan and H. W. Bush administrations. In fact, the United States was the most active country in expanding the convention, initiating seven new articles. This was despite delegates from the Reagan White House signaling the United States was not willing to ratify the final treaty but was interested in making the final agreement better for other countries [26]. When the treaty was opened for signature in 1989, unlike the 195 other countries, the United States refused to sign. It wasn't until 1995, under the Clinton administration, that the United States signed onto the CRC [27]. However, as mentioned above, signing the treaty is largely a symbolic gesture. Ratification requires two thirds of the Senate to vote in favor, and due to strong opposition mainly among conservative members, Clinton never sent the document to Congress. Similarly, President Obama expressed interest in finally ratifying the treaty and asked the Congressional Research Service to review the convention [28]. Unfortunately, it was never submitted to Congress under his administration either.

Opposition to the Convention on the Rights of the Child in the United States

Understanding the broad opposition to a document that most of the world has ratified requires examining some of the prominent lobbying forces in the United States. The Heritage Foundation, a prominent conservative think tank based in Washington D.C., believes that the CRC infringes on parental rights to raise their child, broadly stating that if the government acts "in the best interest of the child" (Article 3), it would supersede the parent's preference for their children [29]. According to the Heritage Foundation, accepting the articles that guarantee the child's right to privacy (Article 16) and freedom of expression (Article 13) would infringe upon the parents' right to imprint their ethics and parental priorities on their children, and the right to social support and childcare (Article 18) would "jeopardize the position of women who want to stay at home to raise their children" [29]. These concerns are shared by the Parental Rights Foundation and other organizations in the parents' rights movement [30]. Additional criticism comes from the Home School Legal Defense Association that claims that ensuring a child's right to education (Article 28) would diminish parents' freedoms to make up their own curriculum when homeschooling [31].

Unfortunately, the reality is that with two thirds of the Senate required to ratify any treaty, there would need to be a bipartisan push to move forward. While the United States in many ways led the initial push for child labor laws and protection, these important gains are under attack. A report by the Economic Policy Institute in 2023 found that 10 states in the United States have introduced bills to weaken childhood labor laws and that many states use a two-tiered labor standards system: one for Americans and one for migrant workers [32]. These bills were introduced by industry groups in a larger bid to weaken federal labor laws. Additionally, the United States has the highest childhood incarceration in the world [33], despite research that shows children who have been in juvenile detention grow up with worse mental and physical health [34]. These health effects disproportionately affect our children of color, with Native American youths being incarcerated at three times the rate of White counterparts and Black children at over four times [35, 36]. While these issues will not be rectified by a ratification of the CRC in and of itself, it would be an important step forward in a time when child rights may be the most vulnerable.

References

1. Heywood C. A history of childhood. 2nd ed. Medford: Polity Press; 2018.
2. Aries P. Centuries of childhood: a social history of family life. New York: Vintage Books; 1965.
3. Sommerville CJ. The discovery of childhood in Puritan England. Athens: University of Georgia Press; 1992.
4. Locke J. Some thoughts concerning education. Standard Ebooks; 2022.
5. Arnett JJ. G. Stanley Hall's adolescence: brilliance and nonsense. Hist Psychol. 2006;9(3):186–97. https://doi.org/10.1037/1093-4510.9.3.186.
6. Watson T. Prehistoric children as young as eight worked as brickmakers and miners. Nature. 2018;561(7724):445–6. https://doi.org/10.1038/d41586-018-06747-w.
7. Caldwell JC. Transmuting the industrial revolution into mortality decline. In: Demographic transition theory. Dordrecht: Springer; 2006. p. 157–80. https://doi.org/10.1007/978-1-4020-4498-4_8.
8. Sinclair U. The Jungle. Upton Sinclair; 1920.
9. Krueger TA, Walter I, Trattner. Crusade for the children: a history of the National Child Labor Committee and Child Labor Reform in America. Chicago: Quadrangle Books. 1970. Pp. 319. $10.00. Am Hist Rev. 1971;76(4):1235. https://doi.org/10.1086/ahr/76.4.1235.
10. Reed AY. Child-labor legislation: a point of view. Elem Sch J. 1922;23(4):276–82.
11. Butchart RE. Freedmen's Education during Reconstruction. In: New Georgia Encyclopedia. 2020. https://www.georgiaencyclopedia.org/articles/history-archaeology/freedmens-education-during-reconstruction/ Accessed 31 May 31, 2023.
12. Schuman M. History of child labor in the United States – part 2: the reform movement. In: U.S. Bureau of Labor Statistics Monthly Labor Review. 2017. https://www.bls.gov/opub/mlr/2017/article/history-of-child-labor-in-the-united-states-part-2-the-reform-movement.htm. Accessed 31 May 2023.

13. West E. "A Right to Childhood": the U.S. Children's Bureau and Child Welfare, 1912–46. By Kriste Lindenmeyer. (Urbana: University of Illinois Press, 1997. xii, 368 pp. Cloth, $49.95, ISBN 0-252-02275-0. Paper, $21.95, ISBN 0-252-06577-8). J Am Hist. 1998;85(1):277–8. https://doi.org/10.2307/2568538.
14. Keating-Owen Child Labor Act (1916). In: National Archives. 2022. https://www.archives.gov/milestone-documents/keating-owen-child-labor-act. Accessed 31 May 2023.
15. Mayer G, Collins B, Bradley DH. The Fair Labor Standards Act (FLSA): an overview, vol 26. Washington, DC: Congressional Research Service; 2013. p. 7-5700, R42713. https://hdl.handle.net/1813/77788
16. United Nations. Vienna Convention on the Law of Treaties 1969. Treaty Ser. 2005;1155:331.
17. Medellín v. Texas, 552 U.S. 491 (2008). Justia U.S. Supreme Court Center. https://supreme.justia.com/cases/federal/us/552/491/
18. Customary international law. In: Cornell Law School Legal Information Institute. 2022. https://www.law.cornell.edu/wex/customary_international_law. Accessed 20 June 2023.
19. Opinio juris (international law). In: Cornell Law School Legal Information Institute. n.d.. https://www.law.cornell.edu/wex/opinio_juris_(international_law). Accessed 20 June 2023.
20. Save the Children. About us. https://www.savethechildren.org.uk/about-us. Accessed 28 June 2023.
21. Geneva Declaration of the Rights of the Child. In: UN Documents: Gathering a body of global agreements. n.d.. http://www.un-documents.net/gdrc1924.htm. Accessed 28 June 2023.
22. UN Declaration on the Rights of the Child (1959). In: Child Rights International Network. 2019. https://archive.crin.org/en/library/legal-database/un-declaration-rights-child-1959.html. Accessed 30 June 2023.
23. Spitz LM. Implementing the U.N. Convention on the Rights of the Child. Vanderbilt Law Rev. 2021;38(3):853–87. https://scholarship.law.vanderbilt.edu/vjtl/vol38/iss3/6
24. United Nations Office of the High Commissioner of Human Rights. International Covenant on Civil and Political Rights. 1996. https://www.ohchr.org/en/instruments-mechanisms/instruments/international-covenant-civil-and-political-rights. Accessed 30 June 2023.
25. UNICEF. A summary of the rights under the Convention on the Rights of the Child. 2016. https://www.unicef.org/montenegro/en/reports/summary-rights-under-convention-rights-child. Accessed 30 June 2023.
26. Cohen CP. The role of the United States in the drafting of the Convention on the Rights of the Child. In: Kilkelly U, Lundy L, editors. Children's Rights. 1st ed. New York: Routledge; 2017. p. 75–88.
27. Convention on the Rights of the Child. In: United Nations Treaty Collection. 1990. https://treaties.un.org/pages/ViewDetails.aspx?src=IND&mtdsg_no=IV-11&chapter=4&clang=_en. Accessed 16 Aug 2022.
28. Blanchfield L. The United Nations Convention on the Rights of the Child, vol. 21. Washington, DC: Congressional Research Service; 2013. p. 7-5700, R40484.
29. Fagan P. How U.N. conventions on women's and children's rights undermine family, religion, and sovereignty. In: The Heritage Foundation. 2001. https://www.heritage.org/civil-rights/report/how-un-conventions-womens-and-childrens-rights-underminefamily-religion-and. Accessed 10 Aug 2022.
30. ParentalRights.org. The convention on the rights of the child is back in Congress. 2020. https://parentalrights.org/convention-on-the-rights-back/. Accessed 10 Aug 2022.
31. Smith JM. What does the future hold for homeschool freedom? In: Home School Legal Defense Association (HSLDA). 2021. https://hslda.org/post/what-does-the-future-hold-for-homeschool-freedom. Accessed 10 Aug 2022.
32. Sherer J, Mast N. Child labor laws are under attack in states across the country. In: Economic Policy Institute. 2023. https://www.epi.org/publication/child-labor-laws-under-attack/. Accessed 12 July 2023.

33. Human Rights Watch. Children behind bars: the global overuse of detention of children. In: World report 2016. https://www.hrw.org/world-report/2016/country-chapters/africa-americas-asia-europe/central-asia-middle-east/north. Accessed 10 Aug 2022.
34. Barnert ES, Abrams LS, Tesema L, et al. Child incarceration and long-term adult health outcomes: a longitudinal study. Int J Prison Health. 2018;14(1):26–33. https://doi.org/10.1108/IJPH-09-2016-0052.
35. Rovner J. Black disparities in youth incarceration. In: The sentencing project. 2021. https://www.sentencingproject.org/publications/black-disparities-youth-incarceration/. Accessed 16 Aug 2022.
36. US Department of Justice Office of Juvenile Justice and Delinquency Prevention. Juveniles in correction: state comparisons. In: Statistical briefing book. 2021. https://www.ojjdp.gov/ojstatbb/corrections/qa08611.asp?qaDate=2019&text=no&maplink=link4. Accessed 16 Aug 2022.

Chapter 2
Rethinking Healthcare for Children – Pivot to Human Dignity

Introduction

In the United States, pediatric healthcare has remarkable strengths. The US boasts many of the best children's hospitals in the world. Pediatric education is top-notch, with a high-quality benchmarking system ensuring excellent expertise of both general and subspecialty pediatricians. This remarkable workforce is complemented by a formidable array of nursing professionals as well as a vast assortment of other healthcare professionals specialized in areas ranging from nutrition, pharmacology, and development to genetic counseling and the care of invasive ventilation in critically ill children. Worldwide, this is one of the largest and most knowledgeable workforces dedicated to the care and cure of children.

Despite these strengths, compared to other industrialized nations, outcomes remain poor while costs remain exceedingly high [1–3]. Key population health markers are in fact worsening in the United States; per capita cost continues to increase in every specialty, and progress in individual care is inconsistent [4, 5]. A 2021 analysis by the Commonwealth Fund compared the performance of US healthcare to 11 other high-income countries. It ranked America last on every single measure, including access to care, equity, and healthcare outcomes. The United States had the lowest life expectancy, worse maternal mortality (twice higher than France and 10 times higher than New Zealand) and infant mortality (twice higher than Australia and Germany), and higher chronic disease burden than any other high-income country. All these outcomes were worse for Latinos, Native Americans, and African Americans in the United States.

These measures suggest the need to explore new ways to conceptualize pediatric healthcare. This report argues that a pivot to human dignity, by appealing to healthcare professionals and leaders, the public, and policymakers alike, can provide the foundation necessary to rethink pediatric healthcare along the principles of children's rights to health. Here, we will review how the concept of human dignity came

K. Sacotte et al., *The Evolution of Global Child Rights*, SpringerBriefs in Public Health, https://doi.org/10.1007/978-3-031-45520-9_2

about and its foundational role in advanced, modern societies. We will examine the relationship between human dignity and the growing relevance of human rights and analyze its role in providing the basis for the concept of children's rights to health.

Brief History of the Concept of Human Dignity

What follows is a brief account of some key moments in the history of human dignity and the related concept of human rights. This history cannot be exhaustive and addresses all existing concerns related to human dignity and human rights. Several groups still struggle to have their dignity recognized and acknowledged in several parts of the world, and many human rights violations will not be directly discussed here. These include individuals self-identified as Lesbian, gay, bisexual, transgender, and queer (LGBTQ) in countries such as Nigeria or Saudi Arabia, ethnic minorities in several countries including India due to the caste system and China for non-Han individuals, or women in Afghanistan. Important human rights violations occurred in the second half of the twentieth century such as the killing fields in Laos and Rwanda, or the genocides during the Kosovo war. The United States has not been immune from significant human rights violations, including the Tuskegee syphilis study (1932–1972) [6], the horrific gynecological research of J. Marion Sims [7], or research studies that violated the Nuremberg Code in several English-speaking countries including the United States [8].

Throughout most of Western history, dignity was a concept associated with privilege and high social status with roots in the Latin term *dignitas* [9]. In the Middle Ages, even within major religious traditions, there was a scant acknowledgment of the value of all people, least of all those at the bottom of the socioeconomic and cultural hierarchy such as slaves and peasants, or children and women. Although some claim that Giovanni Pico della Mirandola, in his fifteenth-century *Oratio De Hominis Dignitate*, made one of the first connections between human dignity and freedom [10], it is probably not until the writings of Immanuel Kant that the intrinsic character of human dignity started to fully emerge. Kant's treatises became focal points in the history of dignity by positing the inherent, intrinsic value of every person. Kant radically argued for the inner *worth* of every human being as a contrast to the *price* ascribed to elements of the material world. Human beings are irreplaceable and therefore cannot be ascribed a price according to Kant.

The profound changes occurring by the end of the eighteenth century resulted from a series of intersecting social and political forces. Building on the principles of the Magna Carta [11], the 1776 Declaration of Independence established the United States as one of the first nations to translate into a collective social agenda the principles comparable to human dignity (then called "natural rights"). Despite not yet recognizing the dignity of all ethnic groups or women, the Declaration of Independence was novel in that it was not based on the long-standing rights of elites and the privileged. Rather, it was based on "the separate and equal station to which the Laws of Nature and Nature's God entitle Man." Moreover, the institution of government itself was set up in new ways:

> … *We hold these truths to be self-evident, that all men are created equal, that they are endowed by their Creator with certain unalienable Rights, that among these are Life, Liberty, and the pursuit of Happiness. – That to secure these rights Governments are instituted among Man, deriving their just powers from the consent of the governed …* (Declaration of Independence, July 4, 1776; National Archives; https://www.archives.gov/milestone-documents/declaration-of-independence#transcript)

The 1789 French Revolution was an additional turning point. France's Declaration of the Rights of Man further strengthened the recognition of the inherent worth of every person. According to the Declaration, "ignorance, neglect or contempt of the rights of man are the sole causes of public misfortunes and governmental corruption," "men are born and remain free and equal in rights," and "the purpose of all political association is the preservation of the natural and imprescriptible rights of man."

While these events were taking place in the West, Hinduism and Buddhism in India and Confucianism in China were largely devoid of any systematic appraisal of the inherent value of the human person outside of specific educational or virtue-based efforts to elevate the person above the average man [12]. However, in the nineteenth and twentieth centuries, these traditions have seen a persistent growth of the appreciation for the worth of the average human person [12].

What Drove the Emergence of the Concept of Human Dignity?

It is remarkable that throughout most of human history, there was no concept of human dignity as something inherent to the worth of every human person. This clearly raises the question of why and how this concept formed and emerged. In addition to the role played by normative ethical theories such as Kantian ethics, at the same time, new events were unfolding and shaping societies in different ways.

At least in part, the concept of human dignity probably arose in response to unprecedented structural changes in societies in the last three centuries. Throughout human history, both in the West and East, travel and communication were challenging, and societies were arranged in relatively closely knit communities. Individual members of these communities, even those at the bottom of the social ladder, found support, comfort, and a sense of belonging. They found their identity. In essence, it was more likely for each person to be valued. Each small community needed the contribution of each of its members for its sustenance and flourishing.

During the last three centuries, travel and communication among different peoples have increased to unparalleled levels. These changes have led to industrial growth and opportunity for personal development including education. This resulted in the disintegration of small communities and the related long-held bonds and resources of support. Common people were more likely to find themselves in an entirely new space of solitude and lack of protection. It was more likely for them to feel not valued by strangers and newcomers. In some ways, claiming a fundamental and inherent value of the human person presented a way of reclaiming a safe space for every individual to facilitate their well-being as well as their continued development and growth.

Human rights, therefore, likely emerged as a human need to bring structure to something that for many centuries was inherent to small community life: the respect and value of each of its members. This is consistent with Jack Donnelly's proposal that human rights are rooted in "structure" rather than "culture" [12]. In this sense, human dignity could be considered a "fundamental principle upon which human rights are built as well as a common, yet extremely varied, thread that links peoples of all beliefs, ethnicities, and regions" [12].

This interpretation and the increasing acceptance of human dignity frameworks around the world suggest that the differential rise of the concept of human dignity is not so much due to different cultures as much as structural factors that are occurring at different speeds in various parts of the globe. In other words, African or Asian cultures are increasingly accepting a human dignity framework not because they are becoming Westernized, but because they are encountering similar problems to Western societies as their social structures are changing, possibly because of Western influences, from closely knit, small communities to a life based on large cities with increased mobility and communication.

Overall, ideals of human dignity accelerated during the first half of the twentieth century after the extreme violence and abuses perpetrated by totalitarian communist and national socialist governments in the World War II. It has only been in the last century that the human dignity of women, children, the disabled, and ethnic minorities has been increasingly recognized and codified in treaties, constitutions, and national laws.

Persistent Uncertainties Regarding the Concept of Human Dignity

Even today, tension and ambiguity persist between a foundational and unconditional character of human dignity and a perfectionist view. Human dignity can be interpreted as an inherent and inalienable attribute of every human person. On the other hand, the perfectionist view of human dignity links human dignity to the development and exercise by human beings of their potential capacities. As a result, this interpretation entails that a human who cannot fully develop these capacities may lack dignity. To address these challenges, some experts such as Gilbert Meilaender suggested separating the notion of human dignity from personal dignity [13]. However, for clarity, we will henceforth use the term "human dignity" in its foundational and unconditional character.

Some scholars agree with Arthur Schopenhauer's assertion that the notion of human dignity is "the shibboleth of all the perplexed and empty-headed moralists" [14] who use it to conceal their lack of substance [15, 16]. In fact, Bacaric and Allan contend that "the concept of dignity is itself vacuous. As a legal or philosophical concept, it is without bounds and ultimately is one incapable of explaining or justifying any narrower interests. … the term is so elusive as to be virtually meaningless" [17]. Chalmers and Ida suggested that "dignity is a fuzzy concept and appeals to dignity are often used to substitute for empirical evidence that is lacking or sound arguments that cannot be mustered" [18].

Not everyone agrees with these positions. Some, following Kant's arguments, see human dignity as an intrinsic worth of every individual, an inherent value inextricably connected with being a human person, a characteristic that cannot be gained or lost by any human being. Others, according to Christian views, base human dignity on the fact that humans are created in God's image. Others still see human dignity as a foundational concept, "a sort of axiom in the system or as a familiar and accepted principle of shared morality" [19]. For them, human dignity is hardly a concept that can be analyzed.

Can We Ground the Right to Health in Human Dignity?

The existing uncertainties in defining the concept of human dignity highlight the challenges in utilizing human dignity as a basis for children's rights to health. Audrey Chapman recently highlighted how, although the right to health has been classically grounded in human dignity, "the precise meaning and requirements behind the term (of human dignity) are elusive" [20]. As a result, she points out, there is "lack of clarity about the foundations of and justification for the right to health," leading to the current challenges in reaching "a consensus about the normative content, scope, and requirements of the right," which has also "hindered efforts by some judiciaries to interpret the right" [20]. Moreover, "the incomplete theoretical framework complicates efforts to set priorities for implementation of the components of the right to health" [20]. These observations emphasize the importance of attempting to provide better clarity on the concept and meaning of human dignity.

Reaching Better Clarity on Human Dignity

Jaco Kruger suggests that "a useful point of entry into the ambiguities surrounding the notion of human dignity may be gained by considering the relation between human dignity and human rights" [21]. Indeed, Jack Donnelly posits that although "the concept of human dignity originally emerged largely separate from the idea of human rights, human dignity is an intermediate concept that links human rights to comprehensive doctrines," [12] intended as foundational moral and/or religious systems of thought. In this sense, Donnelly's position is somewhat like Riley and Bos's contention that human dignity is an "interstitial concept" that is "intended to have a unifying effect on our ethical, legal and political practices" [22]. According to Donnelly, "different comprehensive doctrines provide different accounts of human dignity. But these accounts are sufficiently convergent that they allow human dignity to serve as an accepted principle of shared morality" [12, 19]. Glenn Tinder reminds us that "the dignity of the individual is a cliché, yet it retains surprising force," [23] allowing Donnelly to contend that:

> *... lurking beneath this apparent lack of content is in fact a wide range of powerful specifications of the meaning of human dignity, specifications that despite their differences in detail converge enough to provide a bridge between the body of international human rights law and most of the leading comprehensive doctrines of the contemporary world* [12].

In essence, Donnelly suggests that "some loosely defined but not empty conceptions of human dignity underlie, and thus help to shape, contemporary conceptions of human rights." [12] His conclusion is illuminating:

> *... human rights insist that the inherent worth of human beings must not be left in an abstract philosophical or religious domain but rather must be expressed in everyday life through practices that respect and realize human rights* [12].

Despite these important insights, simply linking human dignity with human rights is unlikely to satisfy the need to clarify the underlying basis for human dignity.

A Richer Meaning for Human Dignity as Gift?

Although the link between human dignity and human rights appears well established, Kruger asks, "if something of a richer meaning of human dignity is not lost through such a close association with the rights of the isolated individual" [21]. He suggests that "an understanding of human dignity in terms of gift exchange will allow for the irreducibly social aspects inherent in the notion to be appreciated complementary to the more objective, factual and individual elements usually associated with human rights" [21].

Like the concept of "the giving of the gift," human dignity appears as an irreducibly social phenomenon; it is something that persons grant each other freely. The notion of human dignity, like the giving of the gift, can equalize the inherent differences that exist between people or even hierarchies in societies. The gift, similar to the acknowledgment of the dignity of the other, locks individuals in what Kruger calls "absolute responsibility" [21]. In this way, by appreciating the social dimension of human dignity, we may be able to better understand its richness and foundational value.

Considering the relational dimension of human dignity, Moshe Halbertal's reflections on the consequences of the denial of human dignity and worth help clarify its remarkable social implications [24]. Halbertal points out that there are three primary means of depriving someone of their dignity. First, making someone feel humiliated, degraded, and helpless through a variety of means including shaming, or treating them as a nobody. In fact, not acknowledging the "existence" of a person can be seen as the highest degree of humiliation. Second, treating someone only as an instrument. In essence, this means not acknowledging someone is a person. Instead of conveying the fundamental truth that each human being is irreplaceable, treating someone as an instrument makes them feel exchangeable like "a thing." Halbertal provides an illuminating example to help us appreciate this concept. He considers what happens when someone dies. The "disappearance" of a human person is typically marked by events such as funerals and/or periods of mourning. If someone dies and there is no acknowledgment that they have passed, this means that they can easily be replaced similar to other "things." Third, even more than making someone an instrument is to make them of "no use" at all. For example, seniors or prisoners treated as "superfluous" represent the essence of the "rejection of the gift," as Halbertal calls it. He also points out how this rejection is often the origin of violence as a perverse way to restore the weight of the person whose gift was rejected.

The Gift of the Human Person as the Foundational Basis of Human Dignity

The question regarding what the foundation of human dignity is has been remarkably difficult to answer. Grounding the concept of human dignity is important on several levels, especially the provision of a more robust foundation for human rights and a clearer justification for these rights, including the right to health. Importantly, the foundation of human dignity needs to be clear and acceptable in different types of societies as well as societies composed of persons who adhere to vastly different foundational doctrines.

Capitalizing on Kruger's reference to bringing together the concepts of human dignity and gift exchange [21], we argue that *the foundation of human dignity is the gift of the human person*. In other words, each person has dignity and irreplaceable value because *each human person is a gift*. To clarify this proposition, we will consider several positions, including religious and philosophical beliefs, and neurosciences.

Some individuals adhere to a religious tradition. For some traditions, God infuses a divine character in human beings because they are created in the image of God. Therefore, each human being is a *gift from God* and has infinite dignity. These traditions clearly provide a foundation for human dignity. For those who do not ascribe to any religious belief, different considerations can help understand how human dignity can be based on the concept of the "gift."

Recent investigations in psychology and neuroscience as well as modern philosophical insight bring once more center stage the uniqueness and worthiness of the human person [25–27]. These analyses show the psychophysical unity of the human person. It is wonderful to realize the distinctiveness of the human person and how the interconnection of body and mind makes humans what they are. The work of Erwin W. Straus highlights the characteristics of the human person and how its distinctive upright posture provides novel and enhanced opportunities to interact with the world, including inanimate and animate entities [25]. Think of the unprecedented ability of humans to collect information that transcends the day-to-day needs. The hands, the Aristotelian "tool of tools," with their immensurable social impact as they enable practical relations with the surrounding world that are not possible for other animals. The human changes in the head and face, which makes smell less important while enhancing seeing and talking/hearing. How sight is not earthbound, and how the human mouth and ears are not limited to the perception of noises to protect from dangers but enable an extraordinary degree of communication. The human form enables, perhaps for the first time among any living organism, "a new kind of relation to the surrounding world." Leon Kass suggests that this relation is:

> *one that admits of a knowing and accurate encounter with things, of genuine and articulate communion and meaningful action between living beings, and of conscious delight in the order and variety of the world's many splendored forms* [26].

While animals are built and instinctually programmed to maximize their day-to-day survival and care, human beings have been afforded the opportunity to go beyond the "here and now." Their psychophysical characteristics enable them to appreciate the infinite beauty around them: the stars in the distant sky, the scent of flowers, the serene view of distant mountain peaks, and the calming sound of waves breaking on the shore. The psychophysical unity of the human person is therefore, as Leon Kass reminds us, "remarkably like and unlike other animals" [26].

An integrated neuro-psycho-physical network makes human persons what they are. An integration that is so "perfect" that even minimal changes would be sufficient to dramatically alter the human experience and, most importantly, what the human person is. Robert M. French codifies this point when he states:

> *Consider, for example, a being that resembled us precisely in all physical aspects except that its eyes were attached to its knees. This physical difference would engender enormous differences in its associative concept network compared to our own.... The moral of the story is that the physical level is not dissociable from the cognitive level* [28].

These insights allow us to fully appreciate the sense of wonder and awe intrinsic to the human person, and therefore to each human person. Such a uniquely integrated living system is irreplaceable and of infinite worth, in essence, a gift.

Realizing and accepting that each human person is a gift enables us to appreciate that every single human being, regardless of their capacities, has incommensurable dignity. In other words, human dignity is the direct and immediate result of accepting the human person as a gift. This is the central point, opening our eyes to the sometimes-hidden reality of each human person possessing exceptional worth. Each person is a gift because each person is here and now without that person having contributed in any way to making the request or choosing to exist. This is indeed what we call a gift, receiving something of value without having searched for or asked for it. Since each human person has a beginning (birth) and an end (death) and cannot be replaced, each human person is “embodied” and “unique,” and therefore their value is incommensurable and absolute. In essence, the gift imparts on all of us what Kruger calls “absolute responsibility” [21] toward the person, therefore providing the basis for the “absolute” dignity of each person, regardless of their abilities.

The concept of “gift” might be hard to conceive in our free-market societies where everything appears to result from the pursuit of self-interest and the goal of personal profit. Despite these challenges, Godbout and Caille still posit that the concept of gift remains central in modern societies [29]. Considering the gift and gift exchange, enables, as Kruger suggests, a “plurivocal interpretation of dignity,” revealing its deeper meaning:

> *an understanding of human dignity in terms of gift exchange will allow for the irreducibly social aspects inherent in the notion to be appreciated complementary to the more objective, factual and individual elements usually associated with human rights* [21].

The gift and gift exchange, with their unique material-symbolic coexistence, point to how human dignity is “bound” to the uniqueness and embodiment of each human person. Gift exchange also emphasizes the essentially “relational” characteristic of human dignity [21]. In this way, the concept of gift exchange, with its ability to bring potentially unequal individuals into a “relational equality,” cannot only help resolve the tension that exists in human dignity between the notions of “status and rank” and “equal worth” but also help ground human dignity as a fundamentally relational event. The logic of the gift, with its perennial awaiting for the giving and returning of the gift without any regard for personal gains as well as the realization of the “finitude of the self,” brings into focus human dignity as “absolute responsibility” [21]. Each human person exists as a psychophysical unity in a specific historical moment and location (embodiment) and will not exist again in this same exact form (uniqueness). Each human person exists without that person having searched or asked for its existence. Therefore, each human person is an embodied and unique gift. This imparts “absolute responsibility” to help protect, preserve, and develop that person not only on that same person but also on all other persons that existed in the past, exist now, or will exist in the future.

Respecting the Dignity of Every Person at the Intersection of Two Opposing Worldviews

The fundamental value of every human person provides a healthy way to interpret reality. Totalitarian philosophies give primacy to the collective at the expense of the worth and dignity of the individual person. On the other hand, an extreme individualistic notion of the human person gives primacy to the egocentric desires of the individual person, even at the expense of the “common good.” Between the two extremes, personalistic frameworks propose that the dignity, worth, and freedom of every person are respected regardless of the iron will of the collective. At the same time, the individual person remains relationally engaged with the other members of the community. In other words, while individualism proposes the success of the person regardless of the possible negative consequences on other persons, and totalitarianism is only worried about the success of the collective, personalist approaches inextricably link the success and well-being of the individual person to the success and well-being of the community they live in. In some ways, this is reminiscent of the Aristotelian virtue ethics of the "golden mean," the middle ground between two extremes.

Grounding Children's Rights to Health in Human Dignity

Each child is a gift, even more, both a present gift and a gift in the making. Children are the future of every generation; they are their hope and promise. They possess an almost unlimited potentiality but are more vulnerable than adults, thus underscoring the responsibility toward the "gift of every child." Children, since they are less able to control their future compared to adults, inspire even greater responsibility. In other words, *the foundation of children's dignity is the gift of the child*. The question then becomes, "How does human dignity provide a justification for the right to health of every child?" In contrast to inanimate objects, children are gifts full of life. Accepting the gift full of life implies being attuned to their needs. The answer then lies in the responsibility of adults to respect the unique and embodied gift each child represents by addressing their well-being and very real needs.

According to Abraham Maslow's hierarchy of needs, the fundamental human needs are physiological, safety and security, love and belonging, self-esteem, and self-actualization needs. Although he embeds health with the other safety and security needs, health is directly linked not only to the basic physiological needs of breathing (clean air), food, water, shelter, clothing, and sleep but also to the needs for safety and security, love and belonging, self-esteem, and self-actualization. Health is a crossroad of most children's needs.

Today, more than ever before, pediatric professionals have robust tools to promote children's health. Given the monumental advances in knowledge and ability to improve health and cure diseases, "health" can be monitored and promoted. Addressing children's health means the absolute responsibility of pursuing the highest attainable health possible for each individual child.

Grounding children's rights to health on human dignity as a result of their incommensurable and irreplaceable gift opens unprecedented opportunities to work toward the well-being of all children. More work will be needed to address priority setting in situations of limited resources and clarify the extent to which healthcare should be provided. Nevertheless, accepting and protecting the gift of the child is the basis to accept the dignity of every child and hopefully helping reimagine US pediatric healthcare.

References

1. Institute of Medicine, National Research Council. In: U.S. health in international perspective: shorter lives, poorer health. Washington, DC: The National Academies Press; 2013. https://doi.org/10.17226/13497.
2. McGough M, Telesford I, Rakshit S, et al. How does health spending in the U.S. compare to other countries? In: Peterson KFF, editor. Health system tracker. 2023. https://www.healthsystemtracker.org/chart-collection/health-spending-u-s-compare-countries-2/
3. Schneider EC, Shah A, Doty MM, et al. Mirror, mirror 2021: reflecting poorly – health care in the U.S. compared to other high-income countries. In: The Commonwealth fund. 2021. https://www.commonwealthfund.org/publications/fund-reports/2021/aug/mirror-mirror-2021-reflecting-poorly
4. Djulbegovic B, Bennett CL, Guyatt G. A unifying framework for improving health care. J Eval Clin Pract. 2019;25(3):358–62. https://doi.org/10.1111/jep.13066.
5. Buntin MB. Confronting challenges in the US health care system: potential opportunity in a time of crisis. JAMA. 2021;325(14):1399–400. https://doi.org/10.1001/jama.2021.1471.
6. Stark L, Greene JA. Clinical trials, healthy controls, and the birth of the IRB. N Engl J Med. 2016;375(11):1013–5. https://doi.org/10.1056/NEJMp1607653.
7. Washington HA. Medical apartheid: the dark history of medical experimentation on Black Americans from colonial times to the present. New York: Anchor Books; 2006.
8. Pappworth MH. Human guinea pigs: a warning. Twentieth Century. 1962;171:67–75.
9. Griffin MT, Atkins EM, editors. Cicero on duties. Cambridge: Cambridge University Press; 1991.
10. Sulmasy DP. Human dignity and human worth. In: Malpas J, Lickiss N, editors. Perspectives on human dignity: a conversation. Dordrecht: Springer; 2007. p. 9–18.
11. Magna Carta. In: National archives. 2019. https://www.archives.gov/exhibits/featured-documents/magna-carta
12. Donnelly J. Human dignity and human rights: research project on human dignity for the Swiss Initiative to Commemorate the 60th Anniversary of the Universal Declaration of Human Rights. 2009.
13. Meilaender G. Human dignity and public bioethics. New Atlantis. 2007;17:33–52.
14. Schopenhauer A. On the basis of morality. Indianapolis: Bobbs-Merrill; 1965.
15. Macklin R. Dignity is a useless concept. BMJ. 2003;327(7429):1419–20. https://doi.org/10.1136/bmj.327.7429.1419.
16. Pinker S. The stupidity of dignity. New Republic. 2008;28(5):28–31.
17. Bagaric M, Allan J. The vacuous concept of dignity. J Hum Rights 2006;5(2):257-270. https://doi.org/https://doi.org/10.1080/14754830600653603
18. Chalmers D, Ida R. On the international legal aspects of human dignity. In: Malpas J, Lickiss N, editors. Perspectives on human dignity: a conversation. Dordrecht: Springer; 2007. p. 157–68.
19. Harris J, Sulston J. Genetic equity. Nat Rev Genet. 2004;5(10):796–800. https://doi.org/10.1038/nrg1454.
20. Chapman A. The foundations of a human right to health: Human rights and bioethics in dialogue. Health Hum Rights. 2015;17(1):6–18.
21. Kruger J. Human dignity and the logic of the gift. S Afr J Philos. 2017;36(4):516–24. https://doi.org/10.1080/02580136.2017.1362930.
22. Riley S, Bos G. Human dignity. In: Encyclopedia of philosophy. 2016. https://iep.utm.edu/human-dignity/
23. Tinder G. Facets of personal dignity. In: Kraynak RP, Tinder G, editors. Defense of human dignity – essays for our times. Indiana: University of Notre Dame Press; 2003. p. 237–45.
24. Halbertal M. Three concepts of human dignity [Internet video]. 2015. https://youtu.be/FyEvREFZVvc
25. Straus EW. Phenomenological psychology. Tavistock Publications; 1966.

26. Kass L. The hungry soul: eating and the perfecting of our nature. Chicago: University of Chicago Press; 1999.
27. Shapiro LA. The mind incarnate. Bradford Books; 2004.
28. French RM. Subcognition and the limits of the Turing test. Mind. 1990;99(393):53–65. https://doi.org/10.1093/mind/xcix.393.53.
29. Godbout JT, Caille AC. World of the gift. Montreal: McGill-Queen's Press; 1998.

Chapter 3
Local Factors Affecting Child Health

The rights of the child as laid out in the Convention on the Rights of the Child (CRC) are seemingly simple and straightforward. Article 1 states, "The child must be given the means requisite for its normal development, both materially and spiritually" [1]. There are, however, complex threats to these rights in the United States and worldwide today.

According to the Centers for Disease Control and Prevention (CDC), "healthy development means that children of all abilities, including those with special healthcare needs, are able to grow up where their social, emotional and educational needs are met" [2]. The social and economic settings in which children are born and raised, known as social determinants of health, can radically affect child development.

What Are Social Determinants of Health

Social determinants of health (SDOH) are the conditions in the environments where people are born, live, learn, work, play, worship, and grow that affect a wide range of health and quality-of-life outcomes and risks. The main categories include:

- Economic stability
- Education access and quality
- Healthcare access and quality
- Neighborhood and built environment
- Social and community context

SDOH vary greatly for children in the United States and globally. The following sections explore the state of child health and development in relation to SDOH in the United States.

K. Sacotte et al., *The Evolution of Global Child Rights*, SpringerBriefs in Public Health, https://doi.org/10.1007/978-3-031-45520-9_3

Economic Stability

In the United States, 1 in 10 people live in poverty, but this burden disproportionately affects children and people of color [3]. Nearly 1 in 7 children live in poverty, and 71% of children living in poverty are children of color [4]. Extensive research has demonstrated that children growing up with household income below the poverty level have worse physical, mental, developmental, and educational outcomes than those growing up in wealthier households [5].

Two frameworks aim to describe the ways in which poverty affects child development. The first emphasizes the material goods necessary for development that are lacking in families living in poverty such as food, safe housing, and adequate medical care [6]. Given the scarcity of these necessary resources, child development and health are hindered. The second framework for understanding the effects of poverty on child development describes how the financial stress on parents decreases their emotional well-being. This in turn leads to decreased engagement with children. Parents' psychological distress and conflict have been linked to harsh, inconsistent, and detached parenting [7]. As parental/caregiver interaction is the primary mode of learning in early childhood, decreased engagement alters development drastically.

So how do we improve economic stability in families to improve child development? Higher basic income, supplemental housing, and food programs have all been proposed to support child development by relieving parental financial stress. Higher income would enable parents to decrease their working hours, thus increasing their presence and interaction with their children at home and perhaps allow them to invest financial resources in educational items such as books [8, 9]. Some anti-poverty programs have also shown that moving families to safer neighborhoods may improve learning environments [3, 10]. Alleviating financial hardships through increased incomes and financial assistance programs can improve child development by both providing developmental resources and improving caregiver–child interactions.

Education Access and Quality

In the United States, all children have access to public education from elementary school through high school. While only 0.5% of primary-school-aged children do not attend school in the United States [11], the quality of this education varies greatly across the country.

Low-quality public schools are more likely to be in neighborhoods with higher rates of poverty. Black and Hispanic students are more likely to attend schools with higher proportions of students below the poverty line [12]. Schools with low-income students have been shown to be correlated with lower resources [13]. Additionally, high schools serving Black and Latino students are less likely to have advanced course options than those serving White students [13]. Studies have also shown that school poverty levels affect student achievement: those in schools with higher rates of poverty are less likely to graduate from high school and go on to higher education [13].

It is important to highlight that preparedness for school varies greatly depending upon the environment in which a child spends their early years. Duncan et al. reported that in 2005–2006, high-income families spent $8000 more on child enrichment activities annually than lower-income families [14]. Many low-income families also do not have the funds to send their children to preschool, further widening the gap of school preparedness. This gap extends through high school and college education: children who do not attend a preschool are less likely to graduate from high school and go to college [15]. Several reports have shown that children without access to books at home and other enrichment activities enter kindergarten with significantly smaller working vocabularies and a lower number of skills than children growing up in high-income households [13].

Various programs have been implemented to increase access to quality education and school readiness among low-income families. Reach Out and Read is a program in which every child receives a book at routine pediatric checkups, and parents are taught the importance of reading in early childhood. This improves access to books and has shown improved language ability and vocabulary in young children participating in the program [16]. In the United States, Reach out and Read has become extremely widespread and reaches 1 in 4 children in low-income families. Other programs have focused on obtaining quality materials, teacher retention, and promoting safe learning environments with smaller classes in low-income schools. A combination of these measures could improve school readiness and performance in our most educationally at-risk youth, and therefore should be advocated for on a country-wide basis.

Healthcare Access and Quality

In the United States and several other countries around the world, healthcare access continues to be poor for many families and children despite maximal healthcare expenditure. Adequate access to healthcare is defined by the Institute of Medicine as "the timely use of personal health services to achieve the best possible health outcomes" [17]. Mediators of healthcare access and quality include financial, racial/ethnic/cultural factors, and location.

In the United States, financial aspects of healthcare access and quality often revolve around insurance. Since much of lifelong health can be affected by events occurring in childhood, all children should have access to reliable and affordable health insurance. The rates of uninsured children dropped from 13.9% in 1997 to 4.5% in 2015 due to a combination of Medicaid coverage, Child Health Insurance Program (CHIP), and the Affordable Care Act. More recently, between 2016 and 2020, there was a significant increase in the proportion of uninsured children (6.1% to 7.2%) and a significant decrease in the proportion of children with adequate and continuous insurance (69.4% to 67.4%) [18]. Thus, in addition to those uninsured, many children have insurance that is not adequate to cover their medical needs or have significant gaps in coverage throughout the year. Gaps in insurance coverage could produce delays in sick childcare or skipping well-child checks altogether. This is demonstrated by a significant decrease in the proportion of children with a consistent source of sick care, from 79.7% in 2016 to 74.7% in early 2020 [18]. These patients were disproportionally made up of children from families near or below the poverty level.

A second major mediator of access to care is the ethnic, racial, and cultural background of a family. Some groups, such as African American and Indigenous communities, have faced discrimination and exploitation from the medical community throughout history [19]. This has led to mistrust in the medical system, with individuals of the Black community less likely to see a primary care physician and more likely to use the emergency room for their care [20]. Additionally, children of minority groups have been shown to have worse health outcomes than White children. For example, Black children are disproportionately affected by asthma and have worse health outcomes than White children. This could be due to asthma disproportionately affecting children living in disadvantaged and polluted urban communities [21].

When assessing healthcare access and utilization, Hispanic or Latino children disproportionately represent children without a usual source of healthcare. In addition to financial barriers, another barrier to healthcare for this population could be the language in which it is delivered. For instance, Cohen et al. found that infants whose parents' primary language was not English were half as likely to receive all recommended preventive care visits compared to infants whose parents' primary language was English [22].

The location in which a child lives is another indicator of the access and quality of healthcare received. Children living in rural areas, nearly 1 in 5 in America, have increased rates of accident-related mortality, worse mental health, and higher rates of obesity [23]. These children have decreased access to primary care providers and subspecialty physicians, which likely contributes to poorer health outcomes. Children living in rural areas are more likely to be publicly insured or uninsured and more likely to live in poverty [23].

There are various US programs in place to mediate disparities in healthcare access for children today. CHIP is a government program that aims to improve access to healthcare services for children. It provides low-cost coverage to children whose families do not qualify for Medicaid. CHIP covers well-child examinations, immunizations, and provides some coverage for sick visits. However, the benefits and enrollment criteria differ by state. The premiums can also be as high as 5% of a family's yearly income, which may be cost prohibitive. Since the initiation of the CHIP program, rates of insured children have increased in the United States.

There are multiple initiatives to improve access to care in rural locations. Programs that incentivize physicians and other healthcare professionals to practice in rural, underserved areas include National Health Services Corps, Public Service Loan Forgiveness, and Indian Health Service Loan Repayment Program. These programs offer loan forgiveness or medical school tuition in exchange for a commitment to working in areas with poor healthcare access. The aim is to bring healthcare professionals to children in communities throughout the United States where providers are scarce.

Telehealth has become critical to decreasing healthcare access disparities in the years since the outbreak of the COVID-19 pandemic. During the pandemic, reimbursement for virtual healthcare visits was rapidly expanded by Medicaid and private insurances alike. Both primary care and subspecialty services have adopted telehealth in recent years, expanding access to millions of children throughout the country. Now, rural children with healthcare needs do not need to travel hundreds of miles to the nearest children's hospital or health center to consult with a subspecialist. Per Curfman et al., telehealth can expand the footprint and breadth of pediatric medical and surgical specialties by bringing expertise to remote and under-resourced areas while efficiently directing patients to the most appropriate care settings [24].

Neighborhood and Built Environment

A child's neighborhood can greatly affect their physical and mental health and impact their safety. Factors that constitute the built environment include crime and violence, access to healthy food, quality and safe housing, and environmental conditions.

Children who live in neighborhoods where violence and crime are common can be affected directly or indirectly by witnessing the crime. Low-income neighborhoods tend to be disproportionately affected by violence and crime. Black children are more likely to live in lower-income areas and thus are more frequently affected by violent crime than White individuals [25]. The stress related to exposure to violent crimes has been linked to asthma, hypertension, cancer, and stroke [26]. Many children lack a safe place to play or exercise due to unsafe neighborhoods, thus decreasing their level of physical activity and negatively impacting their overall health.

Access to healthy foods is also a major concern for children today. Children are disproportionately affected by food insecurity in America, with some states reporting up to 21% of children suffering from food insecurity in 2017 [27]. Communities with food insecurity are more likely to be rural, though a significant number of children affected by hunger live in metropolitan areas as well. Adequate nutrition in childhood is imperative, as inadequate nutrition can hinder brain development, affecting the achievement of developmental milestones and academic performance [27].

While the quantity of food available is important, so is the quality. Food deserts, which are present in many American cities, are areas with poor access to fresh, healthy, and affordable food. Many neighborhoods designated as food deserts lack a grocery store, and thus families are forced to obtain food from convenience stores or fast-food chains that offer low-cost but non-nutritious food. Food deserts are more common in areas with fewer residents, high rates of abandoned houses, and residents with lower education levels, lower incomes, and higher rates of unemployment. All children have the right to healthy food, but this is not currently a reality in America – millions of children lack access to healthy food every day.

Equally as important to child development is stable, safe housing. All children have the right to a safe, loving place to live, which creates a healthy environment in which a child can grow, learn, and explore. Unsafe or unstable housing has profound effects on children's mental health and stress response. Children who live in poor housing conditions (i.e., crowding, clutter, lack of indoor climate control, or presence of hazards) are more likely to experience depression and anxiety and have higher rates of behavioral helplessness [28].

Housing instability has also been linked to worse educational performance. Children living in poor-quality housing or disadvantaged neighborhoods have lower kindergarten readiness scores [29]. Additionally, children experiencing homelessness have higher rates of absenteeism in school, putting them at further risk of falling behind their classmates. Given the worrying consequences of unstable housing on child development and education, the utmost emphasis needs to be placed on ensuring high-quality and safe housing for all children.

There are several programs in the United States to address food insecurity and housing instability, though they have not eradicated these issues entirely. Federal Food Assistance Programs, such as the Supplemental Nutrition Assistance Program (SNAP), provide funds for low-income families to purchase food, while school lunch and breakfast programs supply children with free meals at school. The Special Supplemental Nutrition Program for Women, Infants, and Children (better known as WIC), available to pregnant or breastfeeding women and children under 5 years of age, supplies healthy foods and infant formula to help ensure adequate nutrition in all children in this critical time of brain development. These programs are vital for many families around the country, but they are not comprehensive enough for low-income families to survive off exclusively. There are various state and privately funded programs that aid low-income families in renting subsidized apartments, but the quality and availability are variable. We propose that, to ensure the healthy development of all children, stable food and housing must become a right of all children as laid out in the Convention on the Rights of the Child (CRC).

Social and Community Context

Several previously discussed SDOH are closely related to social and community context, which is defined as the setting in which people live and work, including religious and social relationships. The social and community context in which a child develops can have a profound impact on health, culture, and educational achievement. The most fundamental aspects of social and community context are social cohesion, civic participation, perceptions of discrimination and equity, and incarceration or institutionalization.

Social cohesion is a person's trust and solidarity among a group of people. Studies have shown that neighborhoods with decreased social cohesion and engagement are associated with worse health outcomes. Echeverria et al. found that less socially cohesive neighborhoods were associated with increased depression, smoking, and lack of physical activity [30]. In other studies, increased social cohesion was linked to lower rates of stroke and even death [31, 32]. These outcomes have been found in adults. However, ensuring children live in an environment of social cohesion is similarly incredibly important as social support is well-documented to protect children's mental health.

Civic participation is protective for children and adolescents. Those who participate through civic engagement have higher subsequent education and income levels in adulthood. Adolescents who vote on community initiatives or volunteer in their communities have improved subsequent mental health and health behaviors [33]. Participation in the community should be promoted among children and adolescents, as it can contribute to improved health as well as improved social cohesion in the neighborhood.

Children should live in communities free of discrimination with equity for all individuals. Racial discrimination in childhood has been linked to increased rates of anxiety, depression, and lower overall health scores, especially among minority children [34]. Even exposure to vicarious racism (the secondhand exposure to racial discrimination and/or prejudice directed at another individual) can negatively impact the mood of adolescents, making them less likely to engage in necessary healthy behaviors [35]. To ensure the highest degree of health in all children, racism and discrimination need to be eradicated.

Lastly, the rate of incarceration and institutionalization of the members of a community contributes greatly to the social context that influences child health. When large numbers of a community are incarcerated, many children are left without parents or role models in their homes. The United States has high rates of incarceration, which disproportionately affects Black individuals and communities. Parental incarceration has been tied to poor health outcomes, including anxiety, depression, and decreased healthy behaviors [36, 37]. Parental incarceration contributes to intergenerational carceral exposure, in which the children are more likely to be incarcerated themselves in the future. The United States has one of the highest rates of juvenile incarceration in the world, with up to 50,000 children being held in a juvenile detention center on any given day. This can negatively impact child health and development; children in the juvenile justice system have increased rates of depression, anxiety, and post-traumatic stress disorder [37]. Altogether, high rates of incarceration in a community, both of adults and children, negatively impacts child health. To address these challenges, alternatives to mass incarceration should be explored in the United States, especially when the defendants are parents. This will improve both community cohesion and ensure parental figures can remain in the lives of children.

Conclusion

As demonstrated above, SDOH can drastically affect the health and development of a child. In order for children to develop to their fullest potential, they need safe and encouraging environments, access to healthy food, healthcare, and a supporting and loving home. While there has been progress made toward recognizing how SDOH affect children's health, there are still vast inequities in child health throughout our country and the world. To ensure all children have the rights to health as laid out in the CRC, special attention and resources should be paid to programs promoting a safe, healthy, socially cohesive living environment for all children.

References

1. Convention on the Rights of the Child. In: United Nations Office of the High Commissioner Human Rights Instruments. 1989. https://www.ohchr.org/en/instruments-mechanisms/instruments/convention-rights-child. Accessed 15 Aug 2023.
2. Centers for Disease Control and Prevention. Child development basics In: Child development. 2023. https://www.cdc.gov/ncbddd/childdevelopment/facts.html. Accessed 9 Mar 2023.
3. U.S. Census Bureau. QuickFacts: United States. n.d.. https://www.census.gov/quickfacts/fact/table/US/PST045219. Accessed 11 Dec 2020.
4. Children's Defense Fund. The State of America's Children 2023. https://www.childrensdefense.org/the-state-of-americas-children/. Accessed 10 Mar 2023.
5. National Academies of Sciences, Engineering, and Medicine. Consequences of child poverty. In: A roadmap to reducing child poverty. Washington, DC: The National Academies Press; 2019. https://doi.org/10.17226/25246.
6. Ouellette T, Burstein N, Long D, et al. Measures of material hardship: final report. Washington, DC: Department of Health and Human Services Office of the Assistant Secretary for Planning and Evaluation; 2004. Contract 282-98-0006 (TO#31). https://aspe.hhs.gov/reports/measures-material-hardship-final-report
7. Conger RD, Wallace LE, Sun Y, Simons RL, McLoyd VC, Brody GH. Economic pressure in African American families: a replication and extension of the family stress model. Dev Psychol. 2002;38(2):179–93.
8. Raver CC, Gershoff ET, Aber JL. Testing equivalence of mediating models of income, parenting, and school readiness for White, Black, and Hispanic children in a national sample. Child Dev. 2007;78(1):96. https://doi.org/10.1111/j.1467-8624.2007.00987.x.
9. Bornstein MH, Bradley RH, editors. Socioeconomic status, parenting, and child development. Mahwah: Lawrence Erlbaum Associates Publishers; 2003.
10. Huston AC, Duncan GJ, Granger R, et al. Work-based antipoverty programs for parents can enhance the school performance and social behavior of children. Child Dev. 2001;72(1):318–36. https://doi.org/10.1111/1467-8624.00281.
11. Share of primary-school-age children who are out of school. In: Our world in data. n.d.. https://ourworldindata.org/grapher/Share-primary-school-age-out-of-school. Accessed 7 Mar 2023.
12. Orfield G. Reviving the goal of an integrated society: A 21st century challenge. Los Angeles: The Civil Rights Project/Proyecto Derechos Civiles at UCLA; 2009.
13. O'Day JA, Smith MS. Quality and equality in American education: systemic problems, systemic solutions. In: Kirsch I, Braun H, editors. The dynamics of opportunity in America. Cham: Springer; 2016.

14. Duncan GJ, Murnane RJ. *R*estoring opportunity: the crisis of inequality and the challenge for American education. Cambridge, MA: Harvard Education Press; 2014.
15. Deming D. Early childhood intervention and life-cycle skill development: evidence from head start. Am Econ J Appl Econ. 2009;1(3):111–34. https://doi.org/10.1257/app.1.3.111.
16. Reach Out and Read. Research. In: What we do. 2023. https://reachoutandread.org/what-we-do/research/. Accessed 13 Mar 2023.
17. National Research Council, Institute of Medicine Committee on Children. Health insurance and access to care. In: Edmunds M, Coye MJ, editors. America's children. Washington, DC: National Academies Press; 1998.
18. Lebrun-Harris LA, Ghandour RM, Kogan MD, Warren MD. Five-year trends in US children's health and well-being, 2016–2020. JAMA Pediatr. 2022;176(7):e220056. https://doi.org/10.1001/jamapediatrics.2022.0056.
19. Hostetter M, Klein S. Understanding and ameliorating medical mistrust among Black Americans. In: The commonwealth fund transforming care. 2021. https://doi.org/10.26099/9grt-2b21.
20. Arnett MJ, Thorpe RJ, Gaskin DJ, Bowie JV, LaVeist TA. Race, medical mistrust, and segregation in primary care as usual source of care: findings from the exploring health disparities in integrated communities study. J Urban Health. 2016;93(3):456–67. https://doi.org/10.1007/s11524-016-0054-9.
21. Hill TD, Graham LM, Divgi V. Racial disparities in pediatric asthma: a review of the literature. Curr Allergy Asthma Rep. 2011;11(1):85–90. https://doi.org/10.1007/s11882-010-0159-2.
22. Cohen AL, Christakis DA. Primary language of parent is associated with disparities in pediatric preventive care. J Pediatr. 2006;148(2):254–8. https://doi.org/10.1016/j.jpeds.2005.10.046.
23. Bettenhausen JL, Winterer CM, Colvin JD. Health and poverty of rural children: an under--researched and under-resourced vulnerable population. Acad Pediatr. 2021;21(8S):S126–33. https://doi.org/10.1016/j.acap.2021.08.001.
24. Curfman AL, Hackell JM, Herendeen NE, et al. Telehealth: improving access to and quality of pediatric health care. Pediatrics. 2021;148(3):e2021053129. https://doi.org/10.1542/peds.2021-053129.
25. Sheats KJ, Irving SM, Mercy JA, et al. Violence-related disparities experienced by Black youth and young adults: opportunities for prevention. Am J Prev Med. 2018;55(4):462–9. https://doi.org/10.1016/j.amepre.2018.05.017.
26. American Public Health Association. Violence is a public health issue: Public health is essential to understanding and treating violence in the U.S. 2018. https://apha.org/policies--and-advocacy/public-health-policy-statements/policy-database/2019/01/28/violence-is-a--public-health-issue. Accessed 13 Apr 2023.
27. National Quality Forum. A framework for Medicaid programs to address social determinants of health: food insecurity and housing instability. 2017. https://www.qualityforum.org/Publications/2017/12/Food_Insecurity_and_Housing_Instability_Final_Report.aspx. Accessed 8 Mar 2023.
28. Rollings KA, Wells NM, Evans GW, Bednarz A, Yang Y. Housing and neighborhood physical quality: children's mental health and motivation. J Environ Psychol. 2017;50:17–23. https://doi.org/10.1016/j.jenvp.2017.01.004.
29. Coulton CJ, Richter F, Kim SJ, Fischer R, Cho Y. Temporal effects of distressed housing on early childhood risk factors and kindergarten readiness. Child Youth Serv Rev. 2016;68:59–72. https://doi.org/10.1016/j.childyouth.2016.06.017.
30. Echeverría S, Diez-Roux AV, Shea S, Borrell LN, Jackson S. Associations of neighborhood problems and neighborhood social cohesion with mental health and health behaviors: the multi--ethnic study of Atherosclerosis. Health Place. 2008;14(4):853–65. https://doi.org/10.1016/j.healthplace.2008.01.004.
31. Inoue S, Yorifuji T, Takao S, Doi H, Kawachi I. Social cohesion and mortality: a survival analysis of older adults in Japan. Am J Public Health. 2013;103(12):e60–6. https://doi.org/10.2105/AJPH.2013.301311.

32. Kim ES, Park N, Peterson C. Perceived neighborhood social cohesion and stroke. Soc Sci Med. 2013;97:49–55. https://doi.org/10.1016/j.socscimed.2013.08.001.
33. Ballard PJ, Hoyt LT, Pachucki MC. Impacts of adolescent and young adult civic engagement on health and socioeconomic status in adulthood. Child Dev. 2019;90(4):1138–54. https://doi.org/10.1111/cdev.12998.
34. Anderson AT, Luartz L, Heard-Garris N, Widaman K, Chung PJ. The detrimental influence of racial discrimination on child health in the United States. J Natl Med Assoc. 2020;112(4):411–22. https://doi.org/10.1016/j.jnma.2020.04.012.
35. Cohen A, Ekwueme PO, Sacotte KA, Bajwa L, Gilpin S, Heard-Garris N. "Melanincholy": a qualitative exploration of youth media use, vicarious racism, and perceptions of health. J Adolesc Health. 2021;69(2):288–93. https://doi.org/10.1016/j.jadohealth.2020.12.128.
36. Heard-Garris N, Winkelman TNA, Choi H, et al. Health care use and health behaviors among young adults with history of parental incarceration. Pediatrics. 2018;142(3):e20174314. https://doi.org/10.1542/peds.2017-4314.
37. Heard-Garris N, Sacotte KA, Winkelman TNA, et al. Association of childhood history of parental incarceration and juvenile justice involvement with mental health in early adulthood. JAMA Netw Open. 2019;2(9):e1910465. https://doi.org/10.1001/jamanetworkopen.2019.10465.

Chapter 4
Children's Right to Health in the US Child Welfare System: A Case Study

Introduction

The US child welfare system is ostensibly set up to provide for and protect children's well-being. In reality, however, this system routinely harms the health and well-being of the country's most historically oppressed and under-resourced children and families. Ironically, children taken from their parents into "protective custody" by government child welfare agencies experience some of the worst health outcomes among the US pediatric population, despite being a population over whom the government assumes direct physical control and legal responsibility. This chapter focuses on the US child welfare system as a case study for the ways in which the US government fails to uphold its legal and ethical obligations to protect children's health and well-being, particularly under international frameworks such as those set out in the Convention on the Rights of the Child (CRC). Consistent with the World Health Organization, health is defined in this chapter as, "a state of complete physical, mental and social well-being and not merely the absence of disease or infirmity" [1].

First, the chapter provides background information on the US child welfare system and its obligations regarding health management. Next, it describes the systemic features that bring children into government custody, including institutional and systemic inequities based on poverty and race, which disproportionately undermine the health and well-being of Black children and families. Third, it examines the poor health outcomes of children who have experienced the US child welfare system. Finally, the authors explore the ways in which using a rights-based framework, aligned with international law, is more likely to achieve the highest standard of attainable health for all children – and in particular, those involved with the US child welfare system. The authors argue that such a standard should not only include

K. Sacotte et al., *The Evolution of Global Child Rights*, SpringerBriefs in Public Health, https://doi.org/10.1007/978-3-031-45520-9_4

access to medical care but also address social determinants of health such as access to adequate housing, nutrition, and economic security. For children in the child welfare system, the right to health should also consider the significant and long-term health consequences inherent in family separation.

Overview of Children's Health Management in the US Child Welfare System

The US child welfare system consists of government agencies at the state and local levels mandated to enforce federal and state laws relating to child welfare [2]. These agencies receive reports with claims of child maltreatment, investigate those claims, determine if there is evidence that abuse or neglect occurred, and, when these agencies determine it is warranted, remove children from their homes and place them into the physical and/or legal custody of the state [2]. As of 2021, there were just under 400,000 children and youth in government custody [3].

Once a child welfare agency has separated a child from their parents or caregivers and taken the child into custody, the child welfare agency is legally required to meet that child's health needs [2]. The agency will place the child, depending on individual circumstances, in a relative or nonrelative foster home, a group home, an institution, or supervised independent living. Placement considerations include the child's physical and mental health needs, which might require access to specialized treatment, services, and support [4].

The vast majority of children in the child welfare system are covered by Medicaid, a public health insurance program that provides healthcare coverage to low-income adults, children, pregnant people, elderly adults, and people with disabilities [5]. Medicaid is funded jointly by the states and the federal government, so while each state operates their own Medicaid program, they must meet certain federal requirements in order to receive federal funding [6]. Under federal law, Medicaid is an "entitlement program," meaning that anyone who meets basic eligibility requirements has a right to receive Medicaid healthcare benefits [7]. One group entitled to healthcare coverage is children under the age of 21 whose family income falls below a certain percentage of the federal poverty level [6]. The majority of children in government custody are eligible for Medicaid coverage, either through traditional financial eligibility or because children become categorically eligible through another method – for example, due to eligibility under Title IV-E of the Social Security Act, once that child enters the foster system [8]. Youth who age out of the child welfare system are also eligible to receive Medicaid benefits until age 26 [8]. For these children, Medicaid covers preventative screening and testing to identify children's mental and physical health needs early on and requires states to provide services that are medically necessary to correct or ameliorate the child's mental or physical health conditions [6].

The Design and Structure of the US Child Welfare System Perpetuates Negative Health Outcomes

The health and well-being outcomes experienced by children in the US child welfare system are due in large part to structural features and policy decisions of the system itself. Rather than provide children and families with basic supportive services that would promote overall health and well-being, the child welfare system instead routinely penalizes poverty and the corresponding lack of access to basic services. Child welfare agencies actively investigate and separate families in lieu of providing such basic supports.

There is increasing recognition, both domestically and globally, that health must be addressed broadly and holistically. Both the US Department of Health and Human Services and the World Health Organization have emphasized the importance of considering and promoting the wider conditions that impact an individual's health [9]. These factors are often referred to as "social determinants of health" and include factors such as access to healthcare services, stable housing, adequate nutrition, and sanitation – all of which impact a child's health and overall well-being [9]. The World Health Organization defines social determinants of health as, "non-medical factors that influence health outcomes" [10]. They include, "the wider set of forces and systems shaping the conditions of daily life," such as, "economic policies and systems, development agendas, social norms, social policies and political systems" [10].

Research shows that social determinants of health play an outsized role in determining health outcomes. One study found that up to half of modifiable determinants of health are socioeconomic or environmental factors, as opposed to clinical care, which contributes only 10–20% [11]. The World Health Organization has indicated that social determinants of health account for at least 30–55% of health outcomes [10]. It is particularly important to consider the impact social determinants of health have on children, who are in a sensitive period for physical, emotional, and social development, and for whom early intervention can have lifelong effects [12].

The child welfare system operates contrary to these basic principles of health and well-being. Under its current structures, laws, and policies, child welfare agencies separate children from their parents based on factors related to lack of access to social determinants of health, instead of seeking to provide supports to ensure those prerequisites of health and well-being are met in the home. In the process, child welfare agencies cause tremendous additional trauma, harm, and radical drops in children's health and well-being outcomes, as discussed later in this chapter.

This harm is disproportionately borne by Black children and families. As a consequence of current and historic racism in the United States, including residential segregation, discrimination in labor markets, and implicit and explicit biases, Black children and families are disproportionately represented in under-resourced communities, with Black children, for example, three times more likely to live in poverty than White children [13–18]. In the United States, socioeconomic status and race are so insidiously intertwined that it would be impossible to discuss their relationship to the child welfare system as unrelated to each other. In addition, under-resourced Black communities are, by design, highly surveilled by government systems [15]. Individuals and agencies that could be providing supportive services, including healthcare workers, social service providers, educators, law enforcement officers, and child welfare staff, instead often act as agents of state surveillance [15]. These agents report families and bring children into the child welfare system instead of providing them direct support [15]. The US federal law not only supports but also actively requires this type of mandatory reporting and the penalization of families experiencing poverty and is a tool for perpetuating racial discrimination within the child welfare system.

The Child Welfare System Punishes Families Experiencing Poverty

Data shows that the majority of children who moved into the child welfare system are separated from their families for reasons associated with poverty. Child welfare agencies remove children from their families due to "neglect," a broad and amorphous category that, by definition, primarily operates as a code word for conditions of poverty. Reasons to take a child from their family due to "neglect" can include parents' inability to provide adequate food, housing, or medical care [19]. In 2021, 63% of children separated from their families (130,289 children) were removed solely because of conditions of "neglect," and an additional 9% of children were separated from their families (19,406 children) due to inadequate housing, including homelessness [3]. However, rather than providing support to alleviate these factors related to poverty – along with their correlated impacts on the health and well-being of children and families – child welfare systems instead frequently separate families in the name of child protection.

The US Administration for Children and Families has itself acknowledged that "neglect" removals – including removals for "inadequate housing" or "failure to provide adequate nutrition" – are often the result of families living in conditions of poverty [20]. These conditions of poverty overlap with or exacerbate other issues. For instance, housing instability or spending the majority of one's income on housing can compromise the parent's ability to meet their children's other basic needs. Likewise, the stress of navigating housing instability can impact parents' mental health [21].

Spending on child welfare systems, as opposed to services designed to lift families out of poverty, reflect intentional policy decisions. Despite being the wealthiest nation in the world, the United States has one of the highest rates of child poverty, relative to economically comparable countries, ranking 31st out of 34 of the Organisation for Economic Co-operation and Development (OECD) nations [22]. Although the United States spends similar amounts of money per capita on social services compared to other OECD nations, it spends dramatically less on children and families [23]. Thus, the US "social safety net" does little to address the deeply entrenched structural, economic, and racial inequities that leave families without basic necessities [24, 25]. When the United States does attempt to meet the needs of under-resourced families, such economic prioritization has been extremely successful. For example, in 2021, the US Congress expanded the Child Tax Credit (CTC) for 1 year, in effect increasing the amount of direct cash assistance received by families, as well as increasing the number of families that received it and how often it was disbursed [26]. The CTC expansions were responsible for cutting the US child poverty rate nearly in half, from 9.7% in 2020 to 5.2% in 2021, and lifting three million children above the poverty line [27]. In 2022, however, Congress decided against renewing the program, and roughly four million children fell back into poverty [28]. Research demonstrates that at the time this program ended, food insufficiency rates among households with children increased by 25% [28]. Thus even where programs have been quantifiably shown to increase child well-being and decrease child poverty, they have not remained a priority for federal spending.

The punishment of poverty by child welfare systems is also directly codified into US federal child welfare law. The Child Abuse Prevention and Treatment Act of 1974 (CAPTA) requires that individual states include "neglect" as legal grounds for child welfare involvement [29, 30]. As stated earlier, neglect is commonly defined as a caregiver's failure to provide adequate food, clothing, hygiene, nutrition, shelter, medical care, or supervision [19]. However, in many states neglect definitions contain subjective descriptions of parental acts and do not require evidence of serious harm or imminent risk of serious harm [31]. Additionally, some states include neglect within the definition they provide for abuse rather than classifying it as a distinct term [32]. This ambiguity leaves more room for reporting based on individual bias and moral judgments, resulting in unnecessary scrutiny and over-reporting, as well as biased substantiation of suspected abuse and neglect [33, 34]. These state and federal laws promote and even require the separation of children and families, instead of promoting social services to ensure better health outcomes.

Lack of Access to Health Services Feeds Family Separation

In addition to poverty-based family separation, difficulties in accessing appropriate medical services, particularly mental and behavioral health services, mean that families living with disabilities and mental illness also fall under the scrutiny of the US child welfare system. In 2021, 14% of children separated from their families (28,083 children) were removed due to "physical or emotional illness or disabling condition adversely affecting the caretaker's ability to care for the child" [3]. In the same year, 7% of children separated from their families (15,375 children) were removed due to a child's behavioral problem, while 2% (3,840 children) were removed due to the child's disability [3]. For low-income families, health services are not always available or accessible through state Medicaid programs [35]. And the lack of access to appropriate health services, in particular community mental health services, falls disproportionately on children and young adults from Black and under-resourced families [35]. Here again, lack of access to services is a reason for removal, despite systemic barriers that prevent wide swaths of the US population from attaining basic healthcare.

The Disparate Impact on Black Children and Families in the Child Welfare System

The harms of the US child welfare system on children's health and well-being do not affect all children equally. Black children and families are disproportionately impacted at each stage of the child welfare system. Though Black children make up only around 14% of the US pediatric population, they comprise 22% of the child welfare population [36]. Disturbingly, over half (53%) of Black children will be subjected to a child welfare investigation before they turn 18, compared to only 28% of White children [37, 38].

A child's progression through the child welfare system involves multiple stages and decision points – each a point where bias and institutional racism can affect a child's outcomes. When a child is first reported for potential child abuse, research has shown that mandated reporters are more likely to report Black families than White families [39, 40]. For instance, medical professionals are twice as likely to screen Black infants for maternal drug use as White infants [39, 40]. Black pregnant mothers are four times more likely to be subjected to a toxicology test, even with no reports of substance abuse, than White pregnant mothers [41]. Similarly, once a report of child abuse or neglect is made, case workers have discretion to determine whether a case should be investigated or closed. At this stage, studies have found that Black families are between two and five times more likely than White families to have their cases investigated instead of closed [42]. At the end of an investigation, case workers determine whether to substantiate child maltreatment allegations. Researchers have found that, by the age of 18, roughly 1 in 5 Black children will be the subject of a substantiated child maltreatment report, compared to 1 in 10 White children [43]. Additionally, the "risk scores" used to make removal determinations have been consistently lower in cases of removals involving Black children than in cases involving White children, indicating that Black families are separated at a lower threshold of risk [44]. Once removed from their families, Black children "receive inferior services," "are shuffled to more placements and stay in foster care longer," and are less likely to be either reunified with their family or adopted than White children [45, 46]. Finally, the number of Black children whose relationship to their birth parents is legally terminated is double than that of the general population – averaging a shocking 1 out of every 41 children, compared to 1 out of 100 in the general population [47].

Historically, racial discrimination in other areas has also deeply impacted child welfare system practices that diminish the health and well-being of Black children and families, in particular disproportionate rates of incarceration, as well as racial disparities in economic well-being [48].

The structural racism built into the child welfare system, and the disproportionate harm to the health and well-being of Black children and families, has been increasingly recognized by key government leaders and other institutions. Indeed, the Committee on the Elimination of all Forms of Racial Discrimination (CERD) has directly expressed concern about racial disproportionality in the child welfare system and has recommended that the United States take steps to review its practices and policies in this regard. In 2022, the Committee recognized "… that racial disparities occur at almost every stage of the decision-making process in the child welfare system …" and "… recommends that the State party take all appropriate measures to eliminate racial discrimination in the child welfare system" [49].

President Biden himself acknowledged the detrimental effects of the system on the social determinants of health for families of color. In April 2021, Biden noted that "the enduring effects of systemic racism and economic barriers mean that families of color are disproportionately affected," by the fact that in the child welfare system "poverty is often conflated with neglect" [50]. In August 2022, the American Bar Association adopted Resolution 606, which called on legal professionals to acknowledge the "anti-Black systemic racism within the child welfare system, stemming from the history of slavery in the U.S. and perpetuated by over-surveillance of and under-investment in Black families in America" [51].

Poor Health Outcomes in the Child Welfare System

Despite the purported aim of the US child welfare system to provide for children's "welfare," children's health and well-being metrics decline once they enter government custody. Children who enter the foster system already have risk factors that predispose them to health concerns, including factors associated with poverty or previous exposure to trauma, yet research shows that even accounting for this, rates of mental and physical health needs are higher for children in the foster system compared to children from economically disadvantaged families [52]. Entry into the child welfare system further harms children, through the trauma caused by family separation and entry into the system, as well as risks associated with being in the child welfare system. In addition, studies show that children in child welfare systems often have their mental and physical needs go unmet, including basic medical screening and treatment [53]. The result is that children leaving the child welfare system demonstrate decreased well-being metrics in a myriad of ways.

The American Academy of Pediatrics has concluded that "[c]hildren and adolescents in foster care have a higher prevalence of physical, developmental, dental, and behavioral health conditions than any other group of children" [54]. Almost half of all children in the system suffer from a chronic medical condition, and 70% have at least moderate mental health conditions [55]. Mental and behavioral health concerns are particularly high among youth in child welfare systems. Research has found that between 40% and 60% of children in the system are diagnosed with at least one psychiatric disorder [56]. These rates of health concerns are significantly higher for children in the foster system than their peers in the general population. For example, children in the foster system are two times more likely to have asthma, three times as likely to have hearing or vision problems, five times as likely to have anxiety, and seven times as likely to have depression [52]. Rates of health concerns remain high even controlling for economic vulnerabilities. Research shows that rates of mental and physical health needs are higher for children in the foster system compared to children from economically disadvantaged families who have not entered the system [52].

Moreover, children's mental health is further harmed by the trauma they experience from removal and placement into the system and the resulting separation from their parents, families, and communities. Separating children from their families breaks a critical source of attachment. The American Association of Pediatrics has found that family separation "can cause irreparable harm, disrupting a child's brain architecture and affecting his or her short and long-term health. This type of prolonged exposure to serious stress – known as toxic stress – can carry lifelong consequences for children" [57]. Toxic stress can affect a child's mental and physical health as well as their cognitive functioning – it can even alter their gene expression. Heart disease, immune dysregulation, cancer, depression, anxiety, and post-traumatic stress disorder are just some of the long-term adverse effects of toxic stress on children [58]. Despite this, only a handful of jurisdictions in the United States require that the harm of removal be considered before a child is separated from their family and taken into the system.[1] Importantly, for Black children, the trauma of separation includes not only the disruption of critical family and community attachments but also the potential harm to their sense of individual and cultural identity, particularly within the context of historical and ongoing manifestations of anti-Black racism in the United States.

For most children, the experience of being separated from their family is also unexpected and shocking. Without warning, children are taken from their home or school by strangers, sometimes in the middle of the night, and transported to a new, unfamiliar place. If a family foster home is not immediately available, as they often are not, the child may be placed into a group setting, which has been documented to be harmful to child development [59]. In many state systems, a lack of appropriate family foster homes has resulted in children sleeping overnight in child welfare offices [60] or even in the cars of child welfare caseworkers [61]. The act of separation itself, therefore, can cause additional trauma for many children.

While this chapter focuses on child health and well-being, the harms of separation also impact their parents and reverberate through extended family, friends, and community. Parents and caregivers experience severe trauma from their child's

[1] Washington, D.C., New York, Iowa, and Alaska require courts to assess the harm of removal in deciding whether to separate a child from their family. New Mexico and South Carolina include the harm of removal in their reasonable efforts criteria. Hawaii, Minnesota, Nebraska, and Connecticut have issued policies or agency guidance that emphasize family preservation.

removal or threat of removal. This trauma can impact their identities as parents, resulting in grief and loss, and bring on or exacerbate existing mental health and substance abuse disorders [62].

Many children also experience further trauma and harm while in the "protective custody" of child welfare agencies. Despite the system's stated purpose of protecting children from abuse in their homes, the risk of being abused is significantly higher for children in government custody than it is for children in the general population. One study found that around 1 in 3 children in the child welfare system reported being maltreated while in the system [63]. They also experience a higher risk of exposure to sex trafficking as compared to their peers in the general population [64]. In addition, children in the system often experience high placement instability, moving between multiple placements, which itself causes additional trauma and mental health concerns. Once children are in government custody, child welfare systems are failing to meet their medical needs. For example, one study found that over 40% of children had not received adequate optical or dental care [65]. As many as 68% of children in the child welfare system have not received certain basic childhood vaccinations [65]. Research shows that "three of four children who came to the attention of the child welfare systems because of a child abuse and neglect investigation and who had clear clinical impairment had not received any mental healthcare within 12 months after the investigation." [66, 67] These rates are worse for Black children compared to White children in government custody [68].

There is also significant evidence that children in the child welfare system are overprescribed psychotropic medications, powerful drugs that directly affect chemicals in the brain that help to regulate emotions and behavior [69, 70]. Studies have shown that children in the system are prescribed psychotropic medications three times the rate of other children enrolled in Medicaid and are also more likely to be prescribed more than one psychotropic medication at a time [71]. Children in the system are also more likely to stay on psychotropic medications for longer periods than their similarly situated peers who are enrolled in Medicaid but are not in the system [72]. Psychotropic medications can have serious physical and emotional side effects, and many are untested on children, meaning their full short- and long-term side effects on pediatric patients are still unknown [71].

Failure to appropriately address children's health needs, particularly mental health needs, causes lifelong harm. Studies have found that approximately 60% of children who have been in the foster system have a lifetime prevalence of mental health disorders, and children transitioning from the foster system into adulthood are four times more likely to have a mental health disorder than peers who have not had foster system exposure [73]. Children who have experienced trauma are also more likely to demonstrate behaviors that manifest in impulse control or conduct disorders, behaviors that can lead to other poor lifetime outcomes [73].

The health impacts of entry in the child welfare system are long-lasting. In a child's lifetime, child welfare system intervention increases a child's risks in nearly all aspects of life, impacting key determinants of health and well-being. For example, youth who experienced the system are at significantly increased risk for unemployment and poverty, with around half unemployed by age 24 and 1 out of 4 food insecure [74]. Youth who at one time experienced the system make up around 50% of all homeless young people [75]. Additionally, system-impacted children are three times less likely to graduate from high school and six times less likely to graduate from college or postsecondary education, with only 4% graduating from college [74]. Finally, child welfare system intervention increases a child's risk of criminal legal system involvement in a phenomenon sometimes referred to as the "foster-to-prison pipeline." A shocking 92% of youth in the juvenile justice system are first involved in the child welfare system [76], and approximately 25% of youth who experienced the child welfare system will become involved in the criminal legal system within 2 years of leaving the system [77]. Every year in the United States, over 20,000 young adults who reach the age of 18 (or in some cases, age 21) are cut off from support by the system that separated them from their families, many with no stable family connections, a place to call home, or access to financial resources [78].

For a system that claims to offer "protection," young people who have experienced the child welfare system suffer from significant harm to their mental and physical health outcomes, both in the immediate and in the long term.

The US Child Welfare System Violates Children's Rights to Health Under International Law and Human Rights Frameworks

Under international law, the right to health is a human right. The Universal Declaration of Human Rights, adopted in 1948, states that "[e]veryone has the right to a standard of living adequate for the health and well-being of himself and of his family" [79]. Likewise, the International Covenant on Economic, Social, and Cultural Rights (ICESCR) states that it is "the right of everyone to the enjoyment of the highest attainable standard of physical and mental health" and to "the creation of conditions which would assure to all medical service" [80]. For children, the right to health is specifically set out in the Convention on the Rights of the Child (CRC), which states that children have the right to "the enjoyment of the highest attainable standard of health" [81]. State parties to the CRC must "strive to ensure that no child is deprived of his or her right of access to such healthcare services" [81]. Each of these treaties requires countries to undertake the "progressive realization" of the right to health, meaning that countries must make their best effort to move toward the fulfillment of this right, given their available resources.

Although the United States has signed the CRC and the ICESCR, it has not ratified them, meaning they are nonbinding. However, together with documents like the Universal Declaration of Human Rights, these international agreements reflect the global landscape in terms of the right to health. In addition, the United States does have a binding obligation to uphold the principles of nondiscrimination required by the International Convention on the Elimination of All Forms of Racial Discrimination, which it ratified in 1994.

Critically, the right to health under these international frameworks encompasses not only a right to receive necessary medical services but also to the conditions and services that support the highest standard of attainable health. The Committee on the Convention on the Rights of the Child, the body charged with interpreting the CRC treaty, has clarified in its General Comment No. 15 that children's right to health is an "inclusive right," meaning that children have not only a right to "timely and appropriate prevention, health promotion, curative, rehabilitative and palliative services" but also "a right to grow and develop to their full potential and live in conditions that enable them to attain the highest standard of health" [82]. This standard of health can be achieved "through the implementation of programmes that address the underlying determinants of health" [82]. As discussed earlier in this chapter, these underlying "social determinants of health," defined as "non-medical factors that influence health outcomes" include access not only to adequate healthcare services but also to things such as stable housing, adequate nutrition, and sanitation [10]. Research shows that social determinants of health can actually be more important than direct healthcare services in determining individual health outcomes [83].

The right to health under the CRC, and other international treaties, also includes broader human rights principles such as equality and nondiscrimination. The Committee on the Rights of the Child has indicated that "[a] holistic approach to health places the realization of children's right to health within the broader framework of international human rights obligations" [81]. For example, "[i]n order to fully realize the right to health for all children, States parties have an obligation to ensure that children's health is not undermined as a result of discrimination" [81]. This includes, among others, discrimination based on race, color, sex, language, religion, national, ethnic or social origin, disability, sexual orientation, and gender identity [81]. The ICESCR similarly requires that the right to health be applied without discrimination [80]. In addition, the obligations to avoid racial discrimination and to review and address racial disproportionality by state parties is also more broadly required under the International Convention on the Elimination of all Forms of Racial Discrimination (ICERD), to which the United States is a party.

Here too, the social determinants of health play a critical role in ensuring equity and nondiscrimination. Differing access to the social determinants of health can play an important role in creating and maintaining health inequities. Due to these inequalities, health and well-being follow a "gradient" with those with the lowest socioeconomic position suffering the worst health outcomes [10]. Both the US Department of Health and Human Services and the World Health Organization have emphasized the critical role that addressing social determinants of health plays in mitigating health disparities and inequities [9, 10].

The US child welfare system's failure to uphold children's right to health and well-being is particularly egregious because it occurs in a system where children are in the direct custody and care of the state whose ostensible purpose is to protect children's welfare. Yet, the failures of this system also illustrate a wider violation of the right to health. The right to health, as set out in international agreements, applies to all children (as well as all adults). A more holistic approach to the right to health that focuses on social determinants of health would prioritize services and spending that provide for wider conditions of health. In addition, under international frameworks, the right to health must also be applied, keeping in mind concerns of nondiscrimination and racial equity. Yet, the current spending and policy decisions of the US government do not come close to approaching these international standards. Instead, as exemplified by the child welfare system, US health and welfare policies fail to allocate sufficient resources to the types of holistic services and supports that would actually provide for individual and family well-being and that would address historic inequalities. These policies instead pour resources into largely punitive systems, systems that disproportionally target and harm Black communities.

Conclusion

The child welfare system as a case study illuminates key concepts regarding children's right to health. The United States is deeply failing in its responsibilities to protect its most under-resourced children, as evidenced by the health outcomes for children in the child welfare system. This system not only fails to provide adequate health services for children in its direct care, it forcibly separates families under the guise of child health and well-being and in the process actively harms children's mental and physical health, with disproportionate harm to Black children and families. This case study indicates that any successful efforts to ensure the right to health for children must encompass broader health metrics, including not only access to physical and mental healthcare but also broader social determinants of health such as access to adequate housing, nutrition, and other social services. For children in the child welfare system, the right to health should also consider the significant and long-term health consequences inherent in family separation. Finally, the right to health must be applied in line with broader human rights principles of nondiscrimination and equality.

Acknowledgments The contributors are deeply grateful for the guidance and expertise provided by Angela Burton, Hina Naveed, Shereen A. White, and Sandy Santana in drafting this case study and for the support of Children's Rights.

References

1. World Health Organization. Constitution of the World Health Organization. 1946. https://apps.who.int/gb/bd/PDF/bd47/EN/constitution-en.pdf?ua=1
2. Department of Health & Human Services, Administration for Children and Families, Children's Bureau. How the Child Welfare System Works. 2020. https://www.childwelfare.gov/pubpdfs/cpswork.pdf
3. Department of Health & Human Services, Administration for Children and Families, Children's Bureau. The AFCARS Report #29. 2022. https://www.acf.hhs.gov/sites/default/files/documents/cb/afcars-report-29.pdf

4. Department of Health & Human Services, Administration for Children and Families, Children's Bureau. Treatment Foster Care. In: Child Welfare Information Gateway. https://www.childwelfare.gov/topics/outofhome/foster-care/treat-foster/
5. Centers for Medicare & Medicaid Services. Medicaid. In: Medicaid.gov. https://www.medicaid.gov/medicaid/index.html
6. Medicaid and CHIP Payment and Access Commission. 42 U.S.C. § 1396.
7. Center on Budget and Policy Priorities. Policy basics: introduction to Medicaid. 2020. https://www.cbpp.org/research/health/introduction-to-medicaid
8. Department of Health & Human Services, Administration for Children and Families, Children's Bureau. Health-care coverage for children and youth in foster care – and after. In: Child Welfare Information Gateway. 2022. https://www.childwelfare.gov/pubs/issue-briefs/health-care-foster/
9. Department of Health & Human Services, Office of Disease Prevention & Health Promotion. Social determinants of health. In: Healthy People 2030. https://health.gov/healthypeople/priority-areas/social-determinants-health
10. World Health Organization. Social determinants of health. https://www.who.int/health-topics/social-determinants-of-health
11. Hood CM, Gennuso KP, Swain GR, Catlin BB. County health rankings: Relationships between determinant factors and health outcomes. Am J Prev Med. 2016;50(2):129–35. https://doi.org/10.1016/j.amepre.2015.08.024.
12. Sokol R, Austin A, Chandler C, Byrum E, et al. Screening children for social determinants of health: a systematic review. Pediatrics. 2019;144(4):e20191622. https://doi.org/10.1542/peds.2019-1622.
13. Dettlaff AJ, Boyd R. Racial disproportionality and disparities in the child welfare system: why do they exist and what can be done to address them? Ann Am Acad Pol Soc Sci. 2020;692(1):253–74. https://doi.org/10.1177/0002716220980329.
14. Roberts DE. Child welfare and civil rights. Univ Pennsyl Carey L Sch. 2003;585. https://scholarship.law.upenn.edu/faculty_scholarship/585
15. Baughman C, Coles T, Feinberg J, Newton H. The surveillance tentacles of the child welfare system. Colum J Race L. 2021;11(3):501–32. https://doi.org/10.52214/cjrl.v11i3.8743.
16. Clifford S, Silver-Greenberg J. Foster care as punishment: the reality of 'Jane Crow.' The New York Times. 2017. https://www.nytimes.com/2017/07/21/nyregion/foster-care-nyc-jane-crow.html
17. Semega J, Kollar M, Shrider EA, Creamer J. Income and poverty in the United States: 2019. In: United States Census Bureau. 2020. https://www.census.gov/data/tables/2020/demo/income-poverty/p60-270.html
18. Thomas D, Fry R. Prior to COVID-19, child poverty rates had reached record lows in U.S. Pew Research Center. 2020. https://www.pewresearch.org/short-reads/2020/11/30/prior-to-covid-19-child-poverty-rates-had-reached-record-lows-in-u-s/
19. The Administration on Children, Youth and Families, Foster Care Maintenance Payments, Adoption Assistance, and Child and Family Services. 45 C.F.R. § 1355.
20. Department of Health & Human Services, Administration for Children and Families, Children's Bureau. Civil legal advocacy to promote child and family well-being, address the social determinants of health, and enhance community resilience. 2021. https://www.acf.hhs.gov/cb/policy-guidance/im-21-02
21. Dworsky A. Families at the nexus of housing and child welfare. First Focus. 2014. https://firstfocus.org/wp-content/uploads/2014/12/Families-at-the-Nexus-of-Housing-and-Child-Welfare.pdf
22. Collyer S, Curran M, Garfinkel I, Harris D, et al. A step in the right direction: the expanded Child Tax Credit would move the United States' high child poverty rate closer to peer nations. Columbia University, Center on Poverty and Social Policy. 2022. https://www.povertycenter.columbia.edu/publication/2022/child-tax-credit-and-relative-poverty

23. Tikkanen RS, Schneider EC. Social spending to improve population health – does the United States spend as wisely as other countries? N Engl J Med. 2020;382:885–7. https://doi.org/10.1056/NEJMp1916585.
24. Bach WA. The hyperregulatory state: women, race, poverty, and support. Yale J L Feminism. 2014;25(2):317–40.
25. Burton AO, Mantauban A. Toward community control of child welfare funding: repeal the Child Abuse Prevention and Treatment Act and delink child protection from family well-being. Colum J Race L. 2021;11(3):639–80. https://doi.org/10.52214/cjrl.v11i3.8747.
26. Automatic Benefit for Children Coalition. Letter to President Biden and Members of Congress. 2021. https://www.childrensdefense.org/wp-content/uploads/2021/08/ABC-Coalition-State-and-Local-Community-Organizations-Letter-to-Congress-to-Make-the-Child-Tax-Credit-Expansions-Permanent-August-4-2021.pdf
27. Burns K, Fox L, Wilson D. Expansions to Child Tax Credit contributed to 46% decline in child poverty since 2020. In: Child poverty fell to record low 5.2% in 2021, U.S. census bureau. 2022. https://www.census.gov/library/stories/2022/09/record-drop-in-child-poverty.html.
28. Henderson E. Food insufficiency increased in US households by 25% after expiration of Child Tax Credit payments. In: Children's health watch. 2022.
29. Child Abuse Prevention and Treatment Act. Pub. L. No. 93-247, 88 Stat 4.
30. Besharov DJ. The legal aspects of reporting known and suspected child abuse and neglect. Villanova L Rev. 1978;23(3):458–520. https://digitalcommons.law.villanova.edu/cgi/viewcontent.cgi?article=2180&context=vlr
31. Raz M. Too much reporting, too little service. In: Abusive policies: how the American child welfare system lost its way. Chapel Hill: The University of North Carolina Press; 2020. p. 55–72.
32. GA Code § 19-7-5(b)
33. Raz M. Calling child protective services is a form of community policing that should be used appropriately: time to engage mandatory reporters as to the harmful effects of unnecessary reports. Child Youth Serv Rev. 2020;110(2):104817. https://doi.org/10.1016/j.childyouth.2020.104817.
34. Department of Health & Human Services, Administration for Children and Families, Children's Bureau. Child maltreatment 2019. 2021. https://www.acf.hhs.gov/sites/default/files/documents/cb/cm2019.pdf
35. C.K. v. Bassett. 2:22-cv-01791 (Eastern Dist of NY. 2022).
36. Kids Count Data Center. Child population by race and ethnicity in the United States. In: The Annie E. Casey Foundation. 2022. https://datacenter.kidscount.org/data/tables/103-child-population-by-race
37. Hyunil K, Wildeman C, Jonson-Reid M, Drake B. Lifetime prevalence of investigating child maltreatment among US children. Am J Public Health. 2017;107(2):274–80. https://doi.org/10.2105/AJPH.2016.303545.
38. Edwards F, Wakefield S, Healy K, Wildeman C. Contact with child protective services is pervasive but unequally distributed by race and ethnicity in large US counties. Proc Natl Acad Sci USA. 2021;118(30):e2106272118. https://doi.org/10.1073/pnas.2106272118.
39. Dreyer BP. Racial/ethnic bias in pediatric care and the criminalization of poverty and race/ethnicity – seek and ye shall find. JAMA Pediatr. 2020;174(8):751–2. https://doi.org/10.1001/jamapediatrics.2020.1033.
40. Movement for Family Power, Center for Constitutional Rights, National Advocates for Pregnant Women, et al. Violence against women in the medical setting: an examination of The U.S. foster system. 2019. https://ccrjustice.org/foster-SRVAW
41. Perlman NC, Cantonwine DE, Smith NA. Racial differences in indications for obstetrical toxicology testing and relationship of indications to test results. Am J Obstet Gynecol. 2022;4(1):100453. https://doi.org/10.1016/j.ajogmf.2021.100453.

42. Rolock N, Cryer-Coupet Q, Janczewski C. Measurement issues in identifying and describing racial disproportionality and disparity. In: Dettlaff AJ, editor. Racial disproportionality and disparities in the child welfare system, Child maltreatment, vol. 11. Springer Nature; 2021.
43. Youngman Y, Edwards FR, Wildeman C. Cumulative prevalence of confirmed maltreatment and foster care placement for US children by race/ethnicity, 2011–2016. Am J Public Health. 2020;110(5):704–9. https://doi.org/10.2105/AJPH.2019.305554.
44. Rivaux SL, James J, Wittenstrom K, Baumann D, et al. The intersection of race, poverty, and risk: understanding the decision to provide services to clients and to remove children. Child Welfare. 2008;87(2):151–68.
45. Roberts DE. Torn apart: how the child welfare system destroys Black families – and how abolition can build a safer world. New York: Basic Books; 2022.
46. Center for the Study of Social Policy, Linking Systems of Care, National Council of Juvenile and Family Court Judges. Shifting the Perceptions and Treatment of Black, Native, and Latinx Youth Involved in Systems of Care. 2022. https://cssp.org/wp-content/uploads/2022/01/Shifting-the-Perception-of-Black-Latinx-Native-Youth-in-Systems-of-Care.pdf
47. Guggenheim M. The failure to repeal the Adoption and Safe Families Act will long be a stain on this period of American history. Fam Integr J Q 2022;1(1):54–61. https://publications.pubknow.com/view/752322160/54/
48. Roberts DE. Marginalized mothers and intersecting systems of surveillance: prisons and foster care. In: Ergas Y, Jenson J, Michel S, editors. Reassembling motherhood: procreation and care in a globalized world. New York: Columbia University Press; 2017. p. 185–201.
49. United Nations Committee on the Elimination of Racial Discrimination. Concluding observations on the combined tenth to twelfth reports of the United States of America, Article 43. In: International convention on the elimination of all forms of racial discrimination. 2022. https://docstore.ohchr.org/SelfServices/FilesHandler.ashx?enc=6QkG1d%2FPPRiCAqhKb7yhspzOl9YwTXeABruAM8pBAK1xYN2wdGpGmJxT4qZ%2B%2Fzhl9s68flbQK27IwmDC1j6l212QsTq%2B%2FgbOEik44QlDlYZdvGiNLspvbKJ1mADJtn5a1Ojg9FFaST8zoSlBL%2FEgHQ%3D%3D
50. Biden, JR. A proclamation on national foster care month, 2022. 2022. https://www.whitehouse.gov/briefing-room/presidential-actions/2022/04/29/a-proclamation-on-national-foster-care-month-2022/
51. American Bar Association. Resolution 606 – race and child welfare. 2022. https://www.americanbar.org/groups/public_interest/child_law/resources/attorneys/
52. Turney K, Wildeman C. Mental and physical health of children in foster care. Pediatrics. 2016;138(5):e20161118. https://doi.org/10.1542/peds.2016-1118.
53. Medicaid and CHIP Payment and Access Commission. The intersection of medicaid and child welfare. In: Report to Congress on Medicaid and CHIP. 2015; p. 55–88. https://www.macpac.gov/publication/the-intersection-of-medicaid-and-child-welfare/
54. American Academy of Pediatrics. Fostering health: standards of care for children and adolescents in foster care. 2nd ed. New York: AAP; 2005. https://www.aap.org/en/patient-care/foster-care/fostering-health-standards-of-care-for-children-in-foster-care/
55. Simms MD, Dubowitz H, Szilagyi MA. Health care needs of children in the foster care system. Pediatrics. 2000;106(Suppl 3):909–18. https://doi.org/10.1542/peds.106.S3.909.
56. dosReis S, Zito JM, Safer DJ, Soeken KL. Mental health services for youths in foster care and disabled youths. Am J Public Health. 2001;91(7):1094 9. https://doi.org/10.2105/ajph.91.7.1094.
57. Kraft C. AAP statement opposing separation of children and parents at the border. 2018. https://www.aap.org/en/news-room/news-releases/aap/2018/aap-statement-opposing-separation-of-children-and-parents-at-the-border/
58. Nelson CA, Scott RD, Bhutta ZA, Harris NB, et al. Adversity in childhood is linked to mental and physical health throughout life. BMJ. 2020;371:m3048. https://doi.org/10.1136/bmj.m3048.

59. Dozier M, Kaufman J, Kobak R, O'Connor TG, et al. Consensus statement on group care for children and adolescents: a statement of policy of the American Orthopsychiatric Association. Am J Orthop. 2014;84(3):219–25. https://doi.org/10.1037/ort0000005.
60. Whitehead S. High-needs foster kids sometimes have to sleep in hotels or offices. The pandemic made the problem worse. PBS News Hour. 2022. https://www.pbs.org/newshour/nation/high-needs-foster-kids-sometimes-have-to-sleep-in-hotels-or-offices-the-pandemic-made-the-problem-worse
61. Amon E. Homeless and in foster care: hundreds of Washington youth sleeping in offices, hotel rooms and even cars. The Imprint. 2020. https://imprintnews.org/youth-homelessness/homeless-foster-care-washington-youth-sleeping-offices-hotels-cars/47889
62. Sankaran V, Church C, Mitchell M. A cure worse than the disease? The impact of removal on children and their families. Marq L Rev. 2019;102(4):1163–94. https://repository.law.umich.edu/articles/2055/
63. Wexler R. Abuse in foster care: research vs. the child welfare system's alternative facts.In: Youth today. 2017. https://youthtoday.org/2017/09/abuse-in-foster-care-research-vs-the-child-welfare-systems-alternative-facts/
64. Latzman NE, Gibb D. Examining the link: foster care runaway episodes and human trafficking. OPRE report no. 2020-143. Washington, DC: Office of Planning, Research, and Evaluation, Administration for Children and Families, Department of Health and Human Services; 2020. https://www.acf.hhs.gov/sites/default/files/documents/opre/foster_care_runaway_human_trafficking_october_2020_508.pdf
65. Trivedi A. The harm of child removal. NYU Rev L Soc Change. 2019;43:523–80. https://scholarworks.law.ubalt.edu/all_fac/1085
66. Pecora PJ, White CR, Jackson LJ, Wiggins T. Mental health of current and former recipients of foster care: a review of recent studies in the USA. Child Fam Soc Work. 2009;14:132–46. https://doi.org/10.1111/j.1365-2206.2009.00618.x.
67. Pecora PJ, Jensen PS, Romanelli LH, Jackson LJ, et al. Mental health services for children placed in foster care: an overview of current challenges. Child Welfare. 2009;88(1):5–26.
68. Garland AF, Landsverk JA, Lau AS. Racial/ethnic disparities in mental health service use among children in foster care. Child Youth Serv Rev. 2003;25(5-6):491–507. https://doi.org/10.1016/S0190-7409(03)00032-X.
69. Burton AO. "They use it like candy": how the prescription of psychotropic drugs to state-involved children violates international law. Brooklyn J Int L. 2010;35(2):472–6. https://brooklynworks.brooklaw.edu/bjil/vol35/iss2/5/
70. Franklin SS. Over-medication of psychotropic drugs & African-American girls in foster care: submission to the United Nations High Commissioner for Human Rights. 2015. https://uprdoc.ohchr.org/uprweb/downloadfile.aspx?filename=1639&file=CoverPage.https://brooklynworks.brooklaw.edu/bjil/vol35/iss2/5/
71. Zito JM, Safer DJ, Sai D, Gardner JF, et al. Psychotropic medication patterns among youth in foster care. Pediatrics. 2008;121(1):e157–63. https://doi.org/10.1542/peds.2007-0212.
72. dosReis S, Yoon Y, Rubin DM, Riddle MA, et al. Antipsychotic treatment among youth in foster care. Pediatrics. 2011;128(6):e1459–66. https://doi.org/10.1542/peds.2010-2970.
73. Engler AD, Sarpong KO, Van Horne BS, Greeley CS, et al. A systematic review of mental health disorders of children in foster care. Trauma Violence Abuse. 2022;23(1):255–64. https://doi.org/10.1177/1524838020941197.
74. Courtney M, Hook J, Brown A, Cary C, et al. Outcomes at age 26. In: Midwest evaluation of the adult functioning of former foster youth. Chicago: Chapin Hall at the University of Chicago; 2011. https://www.chapinhall.org/research/midwest-evaluation-of-the-adult-functioning-of-former-foster-youth/
75. National Foster Youth Initiative. Housing and homelessness. 2015. https://nfyi.org/issues/homelessness/

76. Casey Family Programs. Is there an effective model for serving youth involved in both the child welfare and juvenile justice systems? 2022. https://www.casey.org/crossover-youth-practice-model/
77. Jim Casey Youth Opportunities Initiative. Toolkit for Jim Casey youth opportunities initiative sites. 2nd ed. 2013. https://assets.aecf.org/m/resourcedoc/aecf-JimCaseyInitiativeToolkit.pdf
78. The Annie E. Casey Foundation. Child welfare and foster care statistics. 2023. https://www.aecf.org/blog/child-welfare-and-foster-care-statistics
79. United Nations. Universal Declaration of Human Rights Article 25. 1948. https://www.un.org/en/about-us/universal-declaration-of-human-rights.
80. United Nations. International Covenant on Economic, Social and Cultural Rights, Article 2. 1966.https://www.ohchr.org/en/instruments-mechanisms/instruments/international-covenant-economic-social-and-cultural-rights
81. United Nations. Convention on the Rights of the Child Article 24. 1989. https://www.ohchr.org/en/instruments-mechanisms/instruments/convention-rights-child
82. United Nations Committee on the Rights of the Child. CRC/C/GC/15: General Comment No. 15 on the right of the child to the highest attainable standard of health. 2013. https://www.ohchr.org/en/documents/general-comments-and-recommendations/crccgc15-general-comment-no-15-right-child-highest
83. Centers for Disease Control and Prevention. why is addressing social determinants of health important for CDC and public health? 2022. https://www.cdc.gov/about/sdoh/addressing-sdoh.html#:~:text=SDOH%20have%20been%20shown%20to,higher%20risk%20of%20premature%20death

Further Reading

Alexander M. The new Jim Crow: mass incarceration in the age of colorblindness. Rev ed. New York: The New Press; 2012.

Bennett N, Hays D, Sullivan B. 2019 data show baby boomers nearly 9 times wealthier than millennials. In: United States Census Bureau, editor. Wealth inequality in the U.S. by household type. 2022. https://www.census.gov/library/stories/2022/08/wealth-inequality-by-household-type.html

Children's Rights. Fighting institutional racism at the front end of child welfare systems: a call to action to end the unjust, unnecessary, and disproportionate removal of Black children from their families. 2021. https://www.childrensrights.org/news-voices/fighting-institutional-racism-at-the-front-end-of-child-welfare

Movement for Family Power. "Whatever They Do, I'm Her Comfort, I'm Her Protector": how the foster system has become ground zero for the U.S. drug war. 2020. https://www.movementforfamilypower.org/ground-zero

US Department of the Treasury. Racial differences in economic security: housing. 2022. https://home.treasury.gov/news/featured-stories/racial-differences-in-economic-security-housing

Chapter 5
Global Stakeholders in the Evolution of the Rights of the Child

Children are among the most vulnerable groups of people, and many are denied rights based on nationality, gender, or simply the circumstances under which they were born. Despite great progress over the last century, poverty continues to have a profound effect on the world's children, with 1 in 6 living in extreme poverty on less than $1.90 USD per day [1]. Similarly, more than 175 million children are not enrolled in preprimary education, missing a critical investment opportunity and suffering deep inequalities from the start [1]. These challenges are compounded by the increasingly protracted nature of armed conflict, humanitarian crises, and forced displacement of families in areas of extreme political instability. In addition to the direct danger these environments impose on individual children, they perpetuate cycles of inequality that undermine the stability and progress of societies everywhere. Children are the future, and as such every nation and the global society as a whole have a vested interest in expanding the rights and opportunities of children to reach their full potential. Every child has the right to protection, healthcare, and adequate education.

United Nations and UNICEF

On the global scene, the United Nations (UN) plays a vital role in promoting and protecting children's rights worldwide. The UN Convention on the Rights of the Child (CRC) sets out the fundamental rights and freedom of children. In the devastating aftermath of World War II, the United Nations created a new agency to provide basic human needs including food, clothing, and healthcare to children across war-torn Europe [2]. This agency is called the UN International Children's Emergency Fund (UNICEF). UNICEF became a permanent part of the United Nations in 1953 and began its legacy of serving children with a successful global campaign against yaws, a chronic disfiguring childhood infectious disease that can

K. Sacotte et al., *The Evolution of Global Child Rights*, SpringerBriefs in Public Health, https://doi.org/10.1007/978-3-031-45520-9_5

typically be easily treated with penicillin [1]. Following the adoption of the Declaration of the Rights of the Child by the United Nations in 1959, UNICEF became the lead agency for children within the UN system and expanded its focus from primarily healthcare to the defense of the whole child – including rights to protection, shelter, education, and adequate nutrition [3]. In 1965, the organization was awarded the Nobel Peace Prize "for the promotion of brotherhood among nations." UNICEF currently works in more than 190 countries and territories, working collaboratively with government authorities, nongovernmental organizations (NGOs), and local communities to develop and implement child-friend policy change in the fundamental rights of access to healthcare, food, and education.

In 2015, the UN General Assembly formulated The sustainable development goals (SDGs), which are a collection of 17 objectives designed to "serve as a shared blueprint for peace and prosperity for people and the planet, now and into the future." SDGs follow and expand upon the millennium development goals (MDGs), which were agreed upon by governments in 2000 and expired in 2015 [4]. These objectives are zero poverty; zero hunger; good health and well-being; quality education; gender equality; clean water and sanitation; affordable and clean energy; decent work and economic growth; industry, innovation, and infrastructures; reduced inequality; sustainable cities and communities; responsible consumption and production; climate action; life below water; life on land; peace, justice, and strong institutions; and partnerships for the goals. These were adopted by all UN Member States in 2015 to end poverty and build a more peaceful, prosperous world through reduction of inequality by 2030. This is incorporated into the 2030 Agenda for Sustainable Development and is a call to action from all nations in global partnership to create a world where no person is left behind and as such go hand-in-hand with strategies aimed at the realization and protection of child rights [4].

UNICEF is the custodian of 18 SDG indicators that directly relate to and impact children. As such, they support countries in generating and analyzing data for these indicators, including developing international standards and mechanisms for the compilation and verification of national data. This data can then be used to inform governments and other stakeholders of the current progress toward the 2030 goals. For example, goal 1 aims to end poverty in all its forms. For the first time, as part of the SDGs, countries have committed to reducing child poverty specifically. Traditionally, child poverty has been measured as a derivative of household poverty, which can be misleading as households may be considered "nonpoor" by income alone, even when the children suffer from deprivation. In response to this, UNICEF has focused on aiding countries in the design and implementation of child poverty reduction. Together, the United Nations and UNICEF continue to serve as key stakeholders in children's rights through advocacy, education, and global partnerships across the public and private sectors [5].

International Labour Organization

The International Labour Organization (ILO) was formed in 1919 as part of the Treaty of Versailles, which ended the World War I. Its purpose was to promote the belief that sustained universal peace can only be accomplished through the foundation of social justice [6]. The ILO sets international standards on child labor in addition to other fundamental principles such as the right to work. Even in the early years, the ILO played a critical role in addressing child labor with the beginning stages focused on piloting programs in select target countries to demonstrate the feasibility of addressing child labor. Much of this work centered on raising international awareness and developing a new international standard on the worst forms of child labor as defined by the ILO, which include the following:

- Slavery and similar issues such as the trafficking of children, debt bondage, serfdom, and children in armed conflict
- Sexual exploitation (prostitution, pornography, and pornographic performances)
- Involvement in illicit activities or crimes, such as the production or trafficking of drugs
- Work that is likely to harm the health, safety, or morals of children [7]

The ILO has been instrumental in spearheading efforts to build a worldwide movement against child labor. Its International Program on the Elimination of Child Labor (IPEC) was created in 1992, with the goal of progressive and sustained elimination of child labor through the capacity building of high-burden countries to deal with this problem. IPEC is currently operating in 107 countries with 42 countries in Africa, 25 in the Americas, 17 in Asia and the Pacific, 16 in Europe and Central Asia, and 7 from the Arab states. The ILO has worked collaboratively with governments, social partners, and civil society in generating momentum for efforts to address child labor at international conferences. These efforts have resulted in hundreds of thousands of children being withdrawn from work and rehabilitated or prevented from entering the workforce. In addition to this direct action, there have been in-depth research, policy and legal analyses, and program evaluations that have led to a substantial knowledge base of statistical data and methodologies, thematic studies, and guidelines and training materials that can be used to inform other stakeholders of high-priority areas as it pertains to children's rights and child labor [8].

Significant progress has been made towards achieving commitments made under the SDGs including addressing eliminating exploitative practives and ensuring access to quality education for all children. Between 2000 and 2012, the total number of children trapped in child labor decreased from 246 million to 168 million, an over 30% reduction [9].

Together with UNICEF, the ILO published "Child Labor: Global Estimates 2020, Trends, and the Road Forward," which outlines the global progress against child labor as a key stakeholder of SDG target 8.7. Unfortunately, child labor remains a formidable challenge globally, with an estimated 160 million children (10% of the world's population) in child labor at the start of 2020, half of which were in dangerous work environments [10]. This report also found that child labor was more likely to occur in agricultural, rural, or poverty-stricken areas and was more likely to affect boys. Of note, 72% of all child labor occurs within families, primarily on farms or other microenterprises. Child labor, even within the family unit, is also frequently associated with children being out of school, with an estimate of more than 25% of children ages 5–11 out of school, and about 33% of children ages 12–14 engaged in child labor out of school. This further perpetuates the cycle of poverty by imposing constraints on education and opportunities for future employment, productivity, and potential income [10].

While significant progress has been made regarding child labor over the last century, this work remains unfinished, and child labor remains a significant public health issue. Per the ILO, poverty remains the single most significant cause of child labor. Ironically, the persistence of child labor also contributes to and perpetuates the cycle of poverty by depriving children of continued formal education and an upbringing centered on healthy development, thus limiting their potential into adulthood [11]. Additional causes include the rationalizing of child labor under the guise of character building or skill development, poor governance, and other cultural contributions (i.e., preparing the child to take over the parent's job). It must be realized that child labor impairs the normal development and well-being of children. Future work includes addressing the challenge of implementing policies centered on the protection of child labor rights per ILO standards, adopting strategies focused on elevating the standards of education of children and their families and reducing socioeconomic disparities to break the cycle of poverty that perpetuates the perceived need for child labor [12].

Governments

National governments have a crucial responsibility to protect and uphold the rights of their citizens, especially children, within their jurisdictions. They may enact legislation, policies, and programs to safeguard children's well-being and provide essential services such as healthcare, education, and food security. Successful implementation of the Convention on the Rights of the Child depends on the systems in place through which legislation and authority are exercised. Similarly, these governance systems must operate with the goal of equity and beneficence for all if human rights are to be protected. Conversely, without the support of both national and local governmental authorities, sustainable progress toward ensuring the protection of such rights is essentially not possible. In 2011, UNICEF, Save the Children, and the Organization for Economic Co-operation and Development hosted a multinational roundtable on child rights and governance. This aimed to identify collaboration areas between governments and child rights advocates and describe the components of a good government structure and its interaction with the people who must exist to further these goals. In the Summary Conclusions of this meeting, such governance was defined as relying on a set of principles including "transparency, responsibility, accountability, participation, and responsiveness to the needs of the people" [13]. All government and policy influence children's rights, including issues related to resource and taxation allocation. Governments are responsible for providing an environment where children are visible and represented as a group in society during policymaking and program implementation. While policymaking and legislation are a vital step in ensuring the protection of children's rights, effective implementation strategies must include action at the local level. Local governments are key stakeholders in the rights of the child, and the proximity of these entities to the people encourages both accountability and participation. Adequate governance focused on key issues related to children's rights, and the encouragement of child participation at the grassroots level can enhance capacity and inclusivity to deliver appropriate care and service for children [14]. For such legislation to survive, both national and local governments must take on the responsibility of ownership and implementation of child-friendly legislation across party lines and opposing ideologies for the greater good of human rights protection. Governments carry the burden of ensuring that all people, including children, are afforded rights and protections, and that such rights are seen as humanitarian in nature rather than political. There remains a great need for a better understanding of the relationship between governance and child rights through dedicated research and exploration of key areas including financial management and resource allocation, political corruption, educational systems, and climate change [15]. Efforts must continue in bridging the gap between policymaking and practical implementation strategies through partnership and transparency with child rights experts, nongovernmental organizations, and the local communities to empower capacity building and sustainable progress.

Nongovernmental Organizations

Much progress has been made in the realization of children's rights across the globe, including the near complete ratification of the CRC within the UN States (apart from the United States). However, significant gaps remain between the formal recognition of child rights and effective implementation. It is universally recognized that the primary responsibility lies with governments, though in the setting of competing interests, insufficient or inappropriate allocation of resources, or in some cases clear corruption, full realization of child rights has not been achieved [14]. Various international and local nongovernmental organizations (NGOs) have advocated for children's rights and play a significant role in designing, implementing, and often funding programs aimed at protecting child rights. NGOs operate in a variety of legal, political, and societal contexts, which results in a wide variation of work and impact. Some examples of large NGOs include Save the Children, Plan International, World Vision, and Human Rights Watch, all of which are now part of the NGO Group for the Convention on the Rights of the Child [16]. This group's mission is to facilitate the promotion, implementation, and monitoring of the CRC and encourages the formation of national NGO coalitions to become a larger voice and stronger advocate for children's rights. Smaller, local NGOs also play a key role in the mission to promote and protect children through partnering with national and international organizations in the frontline implementation of programs such as health screening camps in remote villages, education in women's reproductive health, and vocational training for marginalized women and children to promote economic opportunity and advancement. NGOs also create an important avenue for raising funds for program implementation through donor contributions that is not otherwise accessible in the government sector.

While NGOs are key stakeholders in the advancement of children's rights, there are inherent challenges to successful and sustainable program implementation. An increase in recognition and resource allocation for NGOs involved in successful child rights programs is necessary from national governments. The opportunity for NGOs to collaborate with national governments in establishing children's rights as a top priority in both policy and legislation will allow such programs to expand their capacity and encourage longer-term sustainability.

Media and Communications

Among the rights of the child, the CRC includes communications rights – the right for children to form their own views and express them without fear of retribution or punishment. In Article 12, it is acknowledged that a child has the right to expression in proceedings that affect the child [2]. Article 13 further expands upon this to include "freedom to seek, receive and impart information and ideas of all kinds, regardless of frontiers, either orally, in writing or in print, in the form of art, or through any other media of the child's choice" [2]. Article 13 also outlines a state's capacity to restrict this right "for respect of the rights or reputations of others or for the protection of national security or of public order, or of public health or morals" [2]. The state also has a role in protecting children's privacy and shielding them from slander and libel. Article 17 adds to this, stating that children should have "access to information from a diversity of national and international sources, especially those aimed at the promotion of his or her social, spiritual, and moral well-being and physical and mental health" [2].

The CRC encourages states to defend children from exploitation or sexual abuse. Under Article 19:

> *States Parties shall take all appropriate legislative, administrative, social and educational measures to protect the child from all forms of physical or mental violence, injury or abuse, neglect or negligent treatment, maltreatment or exploitation, including sexual abuse, while in the care of parent(s), legal guardian(s) or any other person who has the care of the child* [2].

Media organizations play a significant role in raising awareness about children's rights and influencing public opinion. Generally, the role of the media can be seen as a positive one regarding child development and advocacy for their rights. It can shape public discourse and drive positive change through responsible reporting and advocacy.

Following the ratification of the Convention on the Rights of the Child, communication rights have gained the attention of several international groups, such as Save the Children, who developed and published guidelines and practical recommendations and encourage thoughtful consideration within the media on the portrayal of children and their rights. As such, UNICEF commissioned the report "The Media and Children's Rights" to assist journalists and other media professionals to consider how the CRC affects the way children can and should be represented by the media. The purpose is to "generate responsible coverage of children, and the impact of adult behavior and decisions on their lives" while protecting the rights of children [17].

In 1990, the United Nations adopted Guidelines for the Prevention of Juvenile Delinquency (the Riyadh Guidelines), which places responsibility on the media especially in relation to pornography, drugs, and violence [18]. These guidelines affirm the necessity of reducing juvenile delinquency and place the responsibility of child well-being from their earliest stages on the greater community. Additionally, in 2000, the General Assembly of the United Nations adopted two optional protocols into the CRC. One directly addresses the involvement of children in armed conflict, seeking to make it illegal for children to be enrolled in military duty before the age of 18. The International Criminal Court has already agreed that enlisting children under the age of 15 years into military groups is a war crime. The other protocol addresses child trafficking, prostitution, and pornography. At present, states are encouraged, but not required, to ratify these protocols and develop implementation strategies to enact them [17].

In exposing and highlighting abuse, the media can increase public awareness and further explore how exploitation can be stopped. As a key stakeholder in child rights, the overarching principle is that media representation of children and their rights is one of advocacy and awareness, and as such should never put children at risk.

Academia and Research Institutions

Researchers and academics contribute to the understanding of children's rights, provide evidence-based recommendations, and help shape policies and interventions. Children and childhood have been the focus of various forms of research since the early 1900s. The complex nature of the children's rights framework necessitates specific attention to international children's rights in academic research. Articles 43, 44, and 45 in the CRC invite collaboration between the United Nations and researchers to develop data-driven interventions through effective study design, monitoring, and evaluation of programs designed to promote and protect child rights. The effective dissemination of data through various platforms (media, publications, presentations) increases public awareness of the rights of the child, which is the foundation of social change and progress [2]. Universities hold the responsibility to equip those whose future work will impact children (schoolteachers, policymakers and legal specialists, social workers, financial experts) with the fundamental understanding of human and child rights, and work toward bridging the gap between legal knowledge and interdisciplinary practical application.

Children

Finally, children are perhaps the most vital stakeholders in the realization and protection of their rights. Many children do not know about their own rights, and many adults even in highly educated sectors are also unaware of children's rights and the CRC. In a thoughtful review assessing this gap in knowledge, it is clear that children value and want to learn their rights and to feel positive about them [19]. However, to build the foundation needed for children's rights to be implemented, adults need to know and embrace them as well. Interestingly, research has not yet focused on how children may develop into defenders of their own rights [20].The progression of children's rights requires adults (and other children) to be able to first be aware of and fully support children's rights. This may empower children to utilize and uphold their rights and then potentially be able to communicate, shape, and develop human rights in the future. It must be acknowledged that children are complete individuals, and as such occupy their own space within the global society. It is also imperative to remember that we are born as entirely dependent beings, reliant on caregivers and other adults for nurture and protection of our basic needs.

Conclusion

Children are our most vulnerable population, and the cost to our society's future of failing to realize and protect their rights is immeasurable. Above all, children need to be safe, feel safe, share their views with the knowledge that they will be heard and respected. While this chapter covered some key stakeholders in the realization of child rights, we, as individuals and as members of the global community, are all stakeholders in ensuring a safe and nurturing environment for all children so that they may reach their fullest potential in the pursuit of liberty and happiness.

References

1. UNICEF. Child rights and why they matter. https://www.unicef.org/child-rights-convention/child-rights-why-they-matter. Accessed 20 July 2023.
2. United Nations Office of the High Commissioner for Human Rights. Convention on the Rights of the Child. 1996. https://www.ohchr.org/en/instruments-mechanisms/instruments/convention-rights-child. Accessed 27 July 2023.
3. United Nations. Global issues: children. https://www.un.org/en/global-issues/children. Accessed 27 July 2023.
4. UNICEF. Using data to achieve the Sustainable Development Goals (SDGs) for children. https://data.unicef.org/sdgs/. Accessed 10 July 2023.
5. World Health Organization. World health statistics 2021: Monitoring health for the SDGs, Sustainable Development Goals. https://apps.who.int/iris/handle/10665/342703. Accessed 2 Jan 2023.
6. International Labour Organization. Child labour. https://www.ilo.org/global/topics/child-labour/lang%2D%2Den/index.htm. Accessed 5 June 2023.
7. International Labour Organization. The worst forms of child labour. https://www.ilo.org/ipec/Campaignandadvocacy/Youthinaction/C182-Youth-orientated/worstforms/lang%2D%2Den/index.htm. Accessed 20 July 2023.
8. International Labour Organization. About the International Programme on the Elimination of Child Labour (IPEC). https://www.ilo.org/ipec/programme/lang%2D%2Den/index.htm. Accessed 5 June 2023.
9. UNICEF. Child labour data. https://data.unicef.org/resources/dataset/percentage-children-aged-5-14-years-engaged-child-labour-sex-place-residence-household-wealth-quintile/. Accessed 27 July 2023.
10. UNICEF, International Labour Organization. Child labour: global estimates 2020, trends and the road forward. 2021. https://data.unicef.org/resources/child-labour-2020-global-estimates-trends-and-the-road-forward/ Accessed 27 July 2023.
11. Haines A, Sanders D, Lehmann U, et al. Achieving child survival goals: potential contribution of community health workers. Lancet. 2007;369(9579):2121–31. https://doi.org/10.1016/S0140-6736(07)60325-0.
12. Radfar A, Asgharzadeh SAA, Quesada F, Filip I. Challenges and perspectives of child labor. Ind Psychiatry J. 2018;27(1):17–20. https://doi.org/10.4103/ipj.ipj_105_14.
13. UNICEF Innocenti Research Centre. Child rights and governance roundtable: report and conclusions. Florence: Innocenti Publications; 2011. https://www.unicef-irc.org/publications/674-child-rights-and-governance-roundtable-report-and-conclusions.html
14. Vandergrift K. Challenges in implementing and enforcing children's rights. Cornell Int Law J. 2004;32(3):547–53.
15. Spitz LM. Implementing the U.N. Convention on the Rights of the Child. Vanderbilt Law Rev. 2021;38(3):853–87. https://scholarship.law.vanderbilt.edu/vjtl/vol38/iss3/6
16. Theytaz-Bergman L. NGO Group for the Convention on the Rights of the Child. Int J Child Rights. 1995;3:452–4.
17. MediaWise. The media and children's rights. 2010. http://www.mediawise.org.uk/children/the-media-and-childrens-rights/. Accessed 6 June 2023.
18. United Nations guidelines for the prevention of juvenile delinquency: The Riyadh guidelines. In: Save the Children Child Rights Resource Centre. https://resourcecentre.savethechildren.net/pdf/Riyadh-guidelines.docx/. Accessed 27 July 2023.
19. Fairhall N, Woods K. Children's views on children's rights: a systematic literature review. Int J Child Rights. 2021;29(4):835–71. https://doi.org/10.1163/15718182-29040003.
20. Quennerstedt A, Moody Z. Educational children's rights research 1989–2019: achievements, gaps and future prospects. Int J Child Rights. 2020;28(1):183–208. https://doi.org/10.1163/15718182-02801003.

Chapter 6
Conclusion

In addition to exorbitant costs and poor outcomes, the US position on children's health is an anomaly in another regard. The United States is the only country that has not adopted a national framework for securing the rights and well-being of all children. All other member states of the United Nations have done so through ratifying the Convention on the Rights of the Child (CRC) [1]. The 1989 CRC is one of the nine core international human rights treaties whose provisions are binding on the countries that have ratified them. The historical reluctance of the United States to ratify international human rights conventions because doing so might impinge on its sovereignty makes it unlikely that this country will ratify the CRC in the near future [2]. However, even in the absence of ratification of the CRC, it is possible and important to adopt a child rights approach to public policy and to support the principles and norms the CRC embodies. The authors of this commentary believe that to improve children's health and welfare, it is essential that child health professionals promote the child rights framework enumerated in the CRC, particularly its provisions on healthcare, to promote the health and well-being of children.

Benefits to Children's Health and Well-being of Adopting a Human Rights Approach to Healthcare

There are several important benefits of adopting a human rights–based approach to children's health. At the most fundamental level, the adoption of a human rights–based approach would bring a commitment to universal healthcare for children, enabling all children to have access to essential healthcare that is accessible and affordable and at the very least the equivalent of primary care. Improving access to good quality and affordable healthcare would particularly put disadvantaged children on a more level playing field. With the appropriate investment of funds and establishment of health facilities, it would enable child health professionals to

K. Sacotte et al., *The Evolution of Global Child Rights*, SpringerBriefs in Public Health, https://doi.org/10.1007/978-3-031-45520-9_6

provide regular preventive as well as curative care. Universal good-quality healthcare would go a long way to improving children's health status and well-being as well as to helping provide a supportive environment for children.

A human rights–based approach changes the view of children from being passive subjects of adult protection to subjects of rights with the entitlements of having their needs met and their best interests protected. In the process, it vests children with a voice to state their opinions and preferences and a right to be consulted, and when sufficiently mature, to participate in the decisions that impact their health and well-being. In other words, within a human rights framework, children are not objects but become subjects with rights and entitlements. This shift requires healthcare professionals and parents to identify effective means of engaging with children and adolescents according to their specific developmental stage. It means that those caring for them should integrate their feedback throughout the design, development, implementation, and evaluation of the changes and initiatives that are being considered. Making positive changes to children's health requires input from all stakeholders; these become shared responsibilities.

A human rights approach would also infuse a more comprehensive outlook into children's health, bringing more balance between the emphasis placed on physical and mental health. The right to health is a right to achieving the highest attainable standard of both physical and mental health. The COVID-19 pandemic with its significant impact on children's and adolescent's mental well-being has been a stark reminder of the centrality of mental healthcare for the well-being of children and their families [3].

A focus on human rights would also bring greater attention and a greater commitment to providing the basic social, economic, environmental resources, policies, and conditions that shape health, sometimes referred to as the social determinants of health. As an article commemorating the 30th anniversary of the CRC noted, "Since the launch of the CRC, it has become clear that the root causes of child health and well-being are primarily defined by social and environmental determinants" [4]. All too often, medical professionals focus their research and intervention on risk factors that are relatively proximal causes of disease such as diet, exercise, or infectious agents but fail to analyze the root causes of disease. As Link and Phelan suggested in their 1995 seminal report, "Individually-based risk factors must be contextualized by examining what puts people at risk of risks" and "social factors such as socioeconomic status and social support are likely fundamental causes of disease that, because they embody access to important resources, affect multiple disease outcomes through multiple mechanisms and, consequently, maintain an association with disease even when intervening mechanisms change" [5]. Social conditions play a major role in determining health inequalities [6].

The Role of Pediatric Health Professionals

It is important that pediatric healthcare professionals play a leadership role in leveraging human rights to advance children's health and well-being, but for this to happen, it is essential that healthcare practitioners are educated about human rights. The 2019 Lancet Commission on Legal Determinants of Health suggested that "both health graduates and law graduates should be introduced to the basics of international human rights law" [7]. This recognition is rooted in the principles outlined by Susannah Sirkin and colleagues at the nonprofit organization Physicians for Human Rights: "Those who take on the ethical oath to protect and promote human life and health have a unique obligation and contribution to make to human rights" [8].

The American Academy of Pediatrics (AAP) has endorsed the CRC and supports its ratification [9]. A 2010 policy statement of the AAP Council on Community Pediatrics and Committee on Native American Child Health, "Health Equity and Children's Rights," lauds the CRC as a foundational document for future policy implementation noting that "the promotion and protection of children's rights can be used to guide the work of pediatricians as clinicians and child advocates" [10]. We affirm these documents and once again recommend that health professionals, particularly those caring for children, find ways to follow the principles contained in the CRC to find ways to reimagine pediatric healthcare for children in the United States.

The Journal of the American Medical Association (JAMA) Pediatrics stated that the United States faces a pivotal moment of opportunity and risk regarding issues affecting children [8]. We agree with this assessment and the idea that a human rights approach grounded on the concept of human dignity of children can provide a powerful tool to support a developmental ecosystem conducive to children thriving [8]. For that to happen, however, child health professionals, particularly pediatricians, will need to take a leadership role to advance children's rights and the adoption of public policies congruent with children's health and well-being.

References

1. Barnert E, Wright J, Choi C, et al. Reimagining children's rights in the US. JAMA Pediatr. 2022;176(12):1242–7. https://doi.org/10.1001/jamapediatrics.2022.3822.
2. Mehta S. There's only one country that hasn't ratified the convention on children's rights. In: American Civil Liberties Union News & Commentary. https://www.aclu.org/news/human-rights/theres-only-one-country-hasnt-ratified-convention-childrens
3. Theberath M, Bauer D, Chen W, et al. Effects of COVID-19 pandemic on mental health of children and adolescents: a systematic review of survey studies. SAGE Open Med. 2022;10:20503121221086712. https://doi.org/10.1177/20503121221086712.
4. Goldhagen J, Clarke A, Dixon P, et al. Thirtieth anniversary of the UN Convention on the Rights of the Child: advancing a child rights-based approach to child health and well-being. BMJ Paediatr Open. 2020;4(1):e000589. https://doi.org/10.1136/bmjpo-2019-000589.

5. Link BG, Phelan J. Social conditions as fundamental causes of disease. J Health Soc Behav. 1995;Spec No:80–94.
6. Phelan JC, Link BG, Tehranifar P. Social conditions as fundamental causes of health inequalities: theory, evidence, and policy implications. J Health Soc Behav. 2010;51(Suppl):S28–40. https://doi.org/10.1177/0022146510383498.
7. Gostin LO, Monahan JT, Kaldor J, et al. The legal determinants of health: harnessing the power of law for global health and sustainable development. Lancet. 2019;393(10183):1857–910. https://doi.org/10.1016/S0140-6736(19)30233-8.
8. Sirkin S, Iacopino V, Grodin MA, Danieli Y. The role of health professionals in protecting and promoting human rights: a paradigm for professional responsibility. In: Gruskin S, editor. Perspectives on health and human rights. New York: Routledge; 2005. p. 537–48.
9. Haggerty RJ. The Convention on the Rights of the Child: it's time for the United States to ratify. Pediatrics. 1994;94(5):746–7.
10. American Academy of Pediatrics (AAP) Council on Community Pediatrics, AAP Committee on Native American Child Health. Health equity and children's rights. Pediatrics. 2010;125(4):838–49. https://doi.org/10.1542/peds.2010-0235.

Index

K. Sacotte et al., *The Evolution of Global Child Rights*, SpringerBriefs in Public Health, https://doi.org/10.1007/978-3-031-45520-9